I Was Hitler's Chauffeur

'I have portrayed the events related in this book
to the best of my knowledge and conscience. I have omitted
nothing and inserted nothing, but have portrayed the
historical facts as I personally experienced them.'

Erich Kempka

Erich Kempka (1910–1975)

I Was Hitler's Chauffeur

The Memoirs of Erich Kempka

Erich Kempka

Introduction by Roger Moorhouse
Translation by Geoffrey Brooks

Frontline Books, London

I Was Hitler's Chauffeur: The Memoirs of Erich Kempka

This edition first published in 2010 by Frontline Books, an imprint of
Pen & Sword Books Limited, 47 Church Street, Barnsley, S. Yorkshire, S70 2AS
www.frontline-books.com, email info@frontline-books.com

ISBN: 978-1-84832-550-0

Publishing History
Erich Kempka's memoir was first published by Kyrburg (Munich) in 1951 and
was entitled *Ich Habe Adolf Hitler Verbrannt* (*I Cremated Adolf Hitler*). In 1975,
the memoir was re-issued by K.W. Schutz Verlag as *Die Letzen Tage Mit Adolf
Hitler* (*The Last Days With Adolf Hitler*), with extra material by Erich Kern.
It was reprinted in 1991 and 2004 by Deutsche Verlagsgesellschaft GmbH
(Preußisch Oldendorf). *I Was Hitler's Chauffeur* is the first English-language
translation of the expanded edition, and it includes a revised plate section
and a new introduction by Roger Moorhouse.

A CIP data record for this title is available from the British Library.

For more information on our books, please visit www.frontline-books.com,
email info@frontline-books.com or write to us at the above address.

Typeset by Wordsense Ltd, Edinburgh

Printed in the UK by the MPG Books Ltd

Contents

Plates

Frontispiece: Erich Kempka

(plates between pages 80 and 89)

Introduction

ERICH KEMPKA WAS ONE of those silent witnesses who is easily forgotten or overlooked by historians. Born in 1910 in the industrial city of Oberhausen in the Ruhr, he grew up in humble circumstances as one of ten children born to a family descended from Polish immigrants. As a young man, he served an apprenticeship with the DKW vehicle distributors in nearby Essen, before finding a job as a driver for a local newspaper. In those early days of the motor car, it was a choice of career that would serve him well and would propel him to the very heart of coming events.

Already a Nazi party member from 1930, Kempka served as chauffeur to the party's regional leader – or Gauleiter – in Essen, Josef Terboven. Early in 1932, he was recommended by Terboven as a reserve driver for Adolf Hitler's personal motor pool. Accepted for that post, he would also be named as one of the eight original members of Hitler's bodyguard – the *SS-Begleitkommando*.

As Hitler's chauffeur, Kempka journeyed right across Germany. Indeed, as he related, his first action after his appointment was to jump into the Führer's six-litre Mercedes and drive the 480 or so kilometres from Munich to Berlin. During the election campaigns of 1932 – the last year of the Weimar Republic – Kempka accompanied Hitler everywhere, covering an astonishing 132,000 kilometres in crisscrossing the country to meet Hitler's plane and deliver him to his various speaking engagements. At other times, he recalled, there was a more relaxed atmosphere, as Hitler – ever the enthusiast for the motorcar – would sit alongside him, chatting easily and map-reading with a road atlas spread across his knees. The connection thus forged would be the defining relationship of Kempka's life. He developed a 'strong personal bond' with Hitler, which, it seems, was reciprocated. Kempka would be a constant companion, faithful servant and close confidante to Hitler for the next thirteen years, until the collapse of the Third Reich.

From this vantage point, Kempka was naturally well placed to observe Hitler at close quarters and to pass comment, not only on his master's foibles but also on those of many of the individuals that made up Hitler's inner circle, including his private secretary Martin Bormann and his personal physician Dr Theodor Morell. He was also one of the few Germans of that era who were well acquainted with Hitler's long-term mistress Eva Braun. Indeed, it would be Kempka who insisted on carrying Eva Braun's body up from the Reich Chancellery bunker on 30 April 1945, prior to its cremation in what remained of the Chancellery garden.

Kempka was also well placed to comment on other salient events of the Third Reich. 'It's a funny thing', the American prosecutor said of Kempka at Nuremberg, 'that you happened to be everywhere.' He was present, for instance, at the so-called 'Night of the Long Knives', when SA-leader Ernst Röhm and many of his fellows were murdered. Yet, his focus in this book was very much on events at the very end of the war, specifically the circumstances of Hitler's death and his own remarkable escape from the bunker and from Berlin.

It was in this capacity, indeed, that Kempka was to come to the attention of the world. At the Nuremberg Tribunal in the summer of 1946, Erich Kempka took the stand as an eyewitness of those tempestuous last days of the Third Reich. He was called, in the first instance, in the trial *in absentia* of Martin Bormann, whose

defence attorney chose the unusua
could not be charged as he had be
the previous year. In his rather
tribunal, Kempka claimed to ha
have seen Bormann alive, and vi
of the Soviet attack in which th
to have perished. Despite Kemp
of Bormann's survival would persist
spawning numerous unconfirmed sightings in Latin America,
his remains were finally discovered – not far from where Kempka
had last seen him – in 1972.*

providing 'b
fact more
the W
acc

Of course, Kempka would also serve as a witness to another
high-profile death. Though he had not seen Hitler's death itself,
he was nonetheless present in the immediate aftermath and was to
be intimately involved in the circumstances surrounding Hitler's
cremation. That afternoon, he was contacted by Hitler's adjutant
Otto Günsche, who demanded that he bring 200 litres of fuel from
his motor pool to the Reich Chancellery garden. Though he did not
know it at the time, that fuel was to be used to cremate the bodies
of Adolf Hitler and Eva Braun. Kempka would be one of the small
group, who stood that afternoon and watched the two bodies burn.

Naturally, perhaps, this moment was to be one of those that rather
defined Kempka's life. Accordingly, his memoirs, first published in
German in 1951, originally carried the sensational title *Ich Habe
Adolf Hitler Verbrannt* ('I Cremated Adolf Hitler'), before being
toned down somewhat for a 1975 reissue as 'The Last Days with Adolf
Hitler'. That later edition also contained an accompanying text by
one Erich Kern, who was himself a veteran of the *SS-Leibstandarte*
and, by the 1970s, was an extremist, right-wing journalist, with
some rather dubious connections. Kern's text, which was billed as

---

* Bormann's remains were initially identified from memory by Hitler's dentist,
Dr Hugo Blaschke. However, definitive identification came only when a DNA test
was carried out in 1998.

ackground and context' to Kempka's memoir, was in
of an extended and intemperate rant, which railed against
stern Allies and against a generation of historians that –
ording to Kern – had peddled lies and distortions about Hitler
nd the Nazi regime.

Even in the 1970s, Kern's text must have seemed somewhat
close to the knuckle. Yet, to the modern reader, it is faintly
ridiculous – tilting as it does at imagined enemies and insistently
defending the indefensible. For this reason, the editors of this first
English-language edition have made the decision to remove Kern's
original introduction and most of 'background and context' that
accompanied it. The only sections of that original text that have
been retained in the present volume are those that genuinely do
provide a modicum of context to Kempka's recollections of those
dramatic final days during the battle for Berlin. They are presented
here as appendices.

Yet for all Kern's self-righteous bile, Kempka is a genial and
engaging host. Self-deprecating and modest in nature, he also
comes across as surprisingly un-ideological for someone who was
an Obersturmbannführer in the SS.* Of course, it is possible that he
was simply tailoring his memoir to the mores of a post-war audience,
and the association with Erich Kern certainly does not suggest that
Kempka was politically beyond reproach. Yet, one does have to
wonder how ideologically motivated and ideologically shaped he
really was, especially given his Polish ancestry. We cannot know for
sure, but it may well be that his fealty to Hitler was much more that
of servant to master, than that of acolyte to prophet.

Kempka also possessed a good ear for the killer phrase and so
soon became a favourite interviewee for a generation of historians
and documentary film makers. James O'Donnell, for instance,
quoted Kempka's memorable description of Hermann Fegelein

---

* A rank that was equivalent to that of a lieutenant colonel.

having 'his brains in his scrotum' and his remark that when Magda Goebbels was around Hitler one could 'hear her ovaries rattling'. It is colourful quips and observations such as these that help to raise this memoir above the ordinary.

This book is part of a series. Along with Christa Schroeder's *He Was My Chief* and Heinz Linge's *With Hitler to the End*, it forms the third volume of what one might call the 'Household Series'. Taken together, the three books make for tremendously enlightening reading, giving us a precious and fascinating insight into the realities of life in the Nazi inner circle and showing both the dynamics and the petty rivalries of the clique of senior personnel around Hitler.

Crucially, in my opinion, these three memoirs also show us Hitler as the members of his household saw him – not as a ranting political extremist, but as a man. This is not merely an academic exercise or an intellectual parlour game; it should serve as a healthy corrective, reminding us that for all his well-documented extremes, Hitler was nonetheless a man who could inspire loyalty, affection, even love. He could be charming and avuncular; he was a kisser of ladies' hands and seems to have treated his household almost as one would an extended family. As Kempka related, Hitler was not like a 'boss'; rather, he played the role of 'an elder, fatherly friend', someone with whom the members of the household could discuss their 'personal problems and needs'. On their trips together, he recalled, Hitler rarely spoke about politics and even used to bring along a snack for his driver.

Such insights cannot, of course, rehabilitate Hitler or even soften his rightly heinous reputation. But they should at least remind us of his fundamental humanity; remind us that after all is said and done, 'we' are the same as 'him'. We naturally like to think of individuals such as Hitler as a breed apart – something very different from ourselves. Memoirs such as Kempka's, however, remind us most emphatically that this is not the case.

I would lastly like to thank the publisher of these three volumes: Michael Leventhal of Frontline Books, for his vision and inspiration in bringing these 'household' memoirs to an English-speaking audience for the first time. I have no doubt that those thanks will be echoed in time both by general readers and by a generation of historians and specialists.

Roger Moorhouse, 2010

Chapter 1

Hitler Employs Me

E ARLY ON 25 FEBRUARY 1932 a telegram reached me* in my
office at the Gau HQ in Essen. 'Be at the adjutancy, Private
Chancellery, Kaiserhof, Berlin on 26 February 1932,' it read.
My boss, Gauleiter Terboven, had been in Berlin for a Reichstag
sitting over the previous forty-eight hours. Was he behind it? I had
no clue, nor any idea that this despatch was to change the course of
my life, a young man with a world full of possibilities.

After receipt of this telegram I never had a minute to myself. On
the slow train to Berlin, I sat bolt upright on a hard bench in a third-
class compartment. The long journey seemed endless. Feverishly I
reflected but could think of no serious misdeeds I had committed.
Reassured, I began to dream that the cable might offer a favourable
change of direction in my life.

When the train arrived finally at Friedrich-Strasse station in
Berlin, I hurried through the bustle of the great city to Wilhelm-
Platz. For several minutes I stood before the Kaiserhof Hotel,
admiring this imposing modern building, before entering the
vestibule through the revolving door. Ladies and gentlemen,
apparently from the highest part of society, jostled around me.

* Erich Kempka (b. 16.9.1910 Oberhausen, Rhineland; d. 24.1.1975 Freiburg-
Heutingsheim). Electrician after leaving school; 31.3.1930 mechanic at DKW;
1.4.1930 joined NSDAP and SS, employed as driver at Gau Essen; 1.3.1932
entered the Führer's service as chauffeur. Final rank: SS-Obersturmbannführer.
(Translator's Note)

I reported to one of the many staff standing around. He seemed to know what to do with me and signalled for me to follow him through long corridors, over thick, plush carpets. On reaching Wilhelm Brückner's room, I was briefly welcomed by Adolf Hitler's adjutant and told to wait in the hotel lobby. To my surprise I found another thirty men there. After short conversations between us I discovered we had all been summoned to the Kaiserhof Hotel by telegram from all corners of Germany. It was obvious how uneasy we all were. Very quickly we ascertained that each of us was the chauffeur for a leading personality of the NSDAP (Nationalsozialistische Deutsche Arbeiterpartei). Thus we were all to some extent prominent in our own professional calling. It would have to be an extraordinarily important job for us all to have been summoned here. Each man hoped privately that he would be the one to land the unknown position. Finally the call came: 'They are waiting for you gentlemen in Room 135!'

Trailing behind another member of staff we were led into Adolf Hitler's living and work quarters in Berlin. From habit we formed a semi-circle, smallest to the left, tallest at the right. As the smallest, I was on the left flank. My hopes plummeted as I looked at my much taller, well-developed colleagues. Beginning with the tallest, Brückner called us forward individually to be quizzed by Hitler on our technical knowledge and personal details. Finally came my turn. 'Erich Kempka . . . father Ruhr mineworker from Oberhausen, twenty-one years old . . . presently chauffeur for Gauleiter Terboven.' Those were my replies to Hitler's first questions. Then he snapped out rapidly: 'What types of vehicle have you driven? . . . Do you know the 8-litre compressor motor? . . . What is the horse power of this vehicle? . . . Where did you learn to drive? . . . You are on a blind zigzag bend doing eighty kilometres an hour when you see an oncoming car. What are your next actions?' The questions came so quickly that I had to react lightning fast. It was not easy, and I had not expected this man to have such a degree of technical knowledge.

After answering the last question to his apparent satisfaction Hitler offered me his hand.

I was surprised to learn that I had apparently done well in this test. This made me feel elated. Just the idea of driving across the length and breadth of Germany alongside such a man, whom all Germany considered one of the outstanding personalities on the political scene, thrilled me. All the candidates for the job had been through the mill and now waited anxiously for what came next: a disappointment. Hitler addressed us briefly and in his emotional way explained what a responsible post was held by the man at the wheel. It had been a great pleasure for him to have had such a large number of responsible men before him. He left us with a brief salute, not having mentioned why we had been sent for. Brückner explained to us that a second chauffeur was needed to assist Julius Schreck for Hitler's personal service. The man chosen would be notified at the appropriate time. Each of us received fifteen Reichsmarks expenses and were then dismissed.

Now began hours of uncertainty. I wandered around Berlin waiting for the time of my train's departure. The meeting with Adolf Hitler had impressed me deeply. Now that I knew what the vacancy was, I lived in hope but suffered from doubt. It was a relief to climb aboard the train bearing me back to Essen. A few days after my return home I received another telegram: 'On 1 March 1932 report to Rudolf Hess at the Brown House, Munich.' My hopes had been fulfilled! I had been chosen to accompany and chauffeur the man about whom all Germany was talking, Adolf Hitler.

Chapter 2

Thirteen Years in Adolf Hitler's Personal Service

O N ARRIVAL IN MUNICH, I stumbled – still tired from the journey – through the snow with my suitcases towards Brienner-Strasse. On enquiry, a passer-by pointed out where I should go. When I reported to Rudolf Hess's office, I was told they were expecting me at Daimler-Benz in Dachauer-Strasse. I therefore took a taxi and was met there by Schreck, Hitler's personal chauffeur and companion. He gave me a very friendly welcome and immediately began to ask me questions about motoring. The first thing he wanted to know was whether I had ever driven a six-litre Mercedes compressor car. I said no, and at that he led me together with his team to a garage where I was shown a six- to eight-seater open touring car. The mere sight of this vehicle excited my admiration. I had never seen anything like it before. Schreck related the technical details of the giant Mercedes and then opened the bonnet.

Because I was too short to drive the car as standard-equipped, blankets had to be strapped to the seat and adjustments made to give me a clear view from the wheel. I then had to manoeuvre the vehicle out of the garage, and once in the open I had a closer look at the engine and checked the oil and water. Meanwhile Schreck's team had grown to seven. All climbed in: I got behind the wheel and drove the giant to Berlin.

In the Reich capital I was introduced to Hitler again. This time our conversation took on a much more personal character. He wanted to know all about my family relationships, everything about my life and previous employment down to the minutest detail. During this hour there developed in me a strong personal bond of faith in Hitler, which never left me over the long years in which I was constantly in his company.

Once the election campaign for the Reich presidency began, I drove the guests' vehicle, covering enormous distances every day. Our arrival in the towns and villages where Hitler was scheduled to speak was invariably punctual. As soon as he had delivered his speech, we drove on. I envied Schreck and looked forward to the occasional opportunities I had to be with him. After his great oratorical efforts Hitler was always cheerful during the drive and would chat with the driver. One of his kindnesses was to prepare a snack for the chauffeur to ward off tiredness at the wheel. The road map on his knees, Hitler did all the navigating himself, working out the various times to ensure he always arrived on the dot. All the chauffeur had to do was drive safely and keep precisely to the timetable. After we had completed several electioneering speeches in northern Germany, we left Hamburg for Berlin.

Because Schreck had reported sick with food poisoning, Hermann Göring, who used to accompany Hitler on most of his travels at that time, drove in Schreck's place next day. Towards evening we arrived in Stettin. Before Hitler went into the hotel, he ordered me to familiarize myself with the car so that I could relieve Göring and drive that night to Landsberg an der Warthe. Our convoy set off between two and three o'clock in the morning, arriving at Schloss Liebenow a few hours later, to a wonderful welcome. While Hitler made his excuses and went off to rest in his reserved room, we in the personal escort and the guests were served more than we could possibly eat.

I would like to mention at this point that before 1932 Hitler never had a heavy meal. Even after taking over the affairs of State, he lived very modestly and in principle drank no alcohol.

Exceptionally he would allow himself a glass of bitters to prevent the stomach problems that had plagued him since being gassed in the First World War.

After the election campaign had come to its end, we returned to Bavaria, deeply impressed by our experiences. We had covered 12,000 kilometres, a distance I was never to beat in such a short period of time. After our arrival in Munich, Schreck – who had by then recovered – confided that the election campaign had been my period of probation. Hitler had told him that my driving was satisfactory. It would now be my duty to drive Hitler in Munich and its environs, while on longer journeys I would drive the guests' car.

In 1932 I drove 132,000 kilometres, crossing all over Germany by day and night. My life was enriched on these trips by many experiences. I never had the feeling of being on travels with a 'boss', but rather with an elder, fatherly friend. He rarely spoke to me about politics, but said I could and should come to him with my personal problems and needs. He had an understanding and a ready ear for everything. He would always ensure that we drivers had the best accommodation and food on the way, emphasizing: 'My drivers and pilots are my best friends! I entrust my life to these men!'

A new election campaign began. In fourteen days Hitler spoke at about fifty locations. Ever more often the drives crisscrossed Germany from end to end. Where the distances between speaking venues were considerable, aircraft were used for the first time to reach the next appointment as quickly as possible. The constant long drives were eventually too much for Schreck, and so for driving purposes Germany was divided into two regions: Schreck was to be Hitler's chauffeur in the northwest, while I was responsible for covering the rest of the country. In that way the years passed. Even after Hitler became Reich Chancellor my position with him did not change. On all journeys home and abroad, in the air, on the Führer-train or aboard ship I was with him. If not driving his car, I would be his personal guest in his close proximity.

*

On the morning of 16 May 1936 I was summoned to Hitler's apartment on Prinz-Regenten-Strasse in Munich. I found him visibly sad and upset. Briefly he informed me of the sudden death of his long-standing loyal companion Julius Schreck. I was appointed successor to Schreck with immediate effect. At the same time I was nominated head of the Führer's motor pool (*Chef des Kraftfahrwesens des Führers*) and promoted to SS-Sturmbannführer. All rights and duties of my predecessor were transferred to me. The sudden death of Schreck affected me deeply. Ever since the first day, when he had given me such a kindly welcome, I had had much to thank him for. I knew nothing of the illness that befell him on a journey from Berlin to Munich. Immediately he arrived he had been hospitalized with severe meningitis, from which he died shortly afterwards. Fate had therefore afforded me no opportunity to take my leave of him.

For me there now began an exhausting period of special responsibility for someone of my fairly young age. I had to be constantly available for duty. I had hardly any free time for myself any more. The demands made of me grew ever larger. New vehicles had to be built. The garages were too small. Mechanics and other personnel had to be recruited. Additionally I had to keep up with the correspondence, which made demands on my time long after my official working day had ended. Hitler placed great personal trust in me, but he insisted that I complied with his requirements and deadlines precisely and to the letter. This trust was naturally a great stimulant for my ambitions. It was always my pleasure to watch over the new vehicles as they were being manufactured. Under my supervision and in close cooperation with the Daimler-Benz factory not only were the well-known Führer-cars built but also cross-country vehicles for manoeuvres, later used for drives in the mountains and later still well proven during the war.

On one occasion Hitler ordered me to place an experimental vehicle from Daimler-Benz at the disposal of the Berchtesgaden Mountain Rescue. It was to be used in the rescue of two mountaineers on the Watzmann. Only through the use of this vehicle could the men be saved. As a result of this success, other cars of the type were built and donated to the Mountain Rescue.

Vehicles with special bodywork were always under construction under my supervision, as gifts from Hitler to foreign Heads of State. Repeatedly I would visit the factory to check how assembly was proceeding and ensure that all extra features were being fitted. Only rarely did I have more than a day for this task, and I would often have to work through the night to keep abreast of my other duties. Hitler required me to keep him permanently informed about the progress of these cars at the works, just as he interested himself especially in all technical matters and innovations.

When the opportunity presented itself I suggested he should have a bullet-proof car built for himself. He turned this idea down at once. His life was in no danger from the German people! Even foreign powers were hardly likely to try to assassinate him! He was convinced that it was known abroad how much he was needed for the development of Europe.

I was taken by surprise when war came. As head of the Führer's motor pool I was not at all prepared for it. Now the idea of the bullet-proof car began to dominate my thinking day and night. Despite Hitler's refusal to have one, in 1939 I had an open-topped example built, on my own initiative. Apart from the armour plating it was no different to any of the related types. I applied to Martin Bormann, who was in charge of the motor pool budget, for finance, but he declined to foot the bill since he knew that Hitler considered armour unnecessary. Thus I was forced to seek donations from wealthy friends to pay for the completed vehicle.

On 8 November 1939 at the Bürgerbräukeller in Munich an attempt was made to assassinate Hitler. This provided me with the excuse to draw his attention to the existence of my bullet-proof car. On the drive from Berlin Anhalter station to the Reich Chancellery I managed to obtain his agreement at least to look at it. Once in the Chancellery I had the new vehicle driven to the portico. Hitler looked it over with great satisfaction while I explained to him the strength of the armour. The windshields were of 45-mm multi-layer glass, the side armour 3.5–4-mm, specially hardened armour plating, while the floor had 9–11-mm plate as protection against land mines or bombs. The car was bullet proof against hand guns and explosives up to about half a kilogram of dynamite. 'In future I will use only this car, for I can never know when some idiot might throw another bomb in front of my vehicle,' Hitler remarked to Bormann with a smile. Bormann now had to pay for the vehicle.

A short while later, without any bodyguard, I made a night drive across the capital in a Volkswagen with Hitler. He liked to make these night outings to give him the best opportunity to observe and inspect the architecture of Berlin while in mufti. Although it is not the purpose of my memoirs to address political questions, I have never forgotten the conversation we had that night. When we stopped at the half-finished Tourist Office on the Potsdamer-Brücke, Hitler said to me: 'What a pity we have this war. In a few years Berlin and many other cities of the Reich would have been rebuilt.'

The boss was enthusiastic about my new bullet-proof car. I was given orders to commission several more. I considered it to be a special recognition of my initiative to receive the honour later of delivering the new vehicles personally to various Heads of State as gifts. Thus in December 1941 I handed over to Baron von Mannerheim, the Finnish leader, an armoured open Daimler-Benz 150 touring car. During my stay in Finland I noticed the poor nutrition of the

Finnish population. Upon my return to Führer-HQ at Rastenburg, East Prussia, I drew the matter of Finland's food shortage to the attention of the Führer. He ordered that 50,000 tonnes of cereals should be made available to the Finnish government.

To mark the seventy-fifth birthday of the Finnish Head of State I received the unexpected order to procure three cross-country vehicles. I succeeded at very short notice in obtaining these from the firm of Steyr. They were loaded at Stettin and shipped to Finland. On Mannerheim's birthday, Hitler flew to Finland. I brought up the cross-country vehicles and Hitler gave them to von Mannerheim as a birthday present.

In January 1942, while the Romanian Head of State, Ion Antonescu, was confined to bed with a severe bout of influenza, I arrived in Bucharest with an armoured limousine. Antonescu was notified of my arrival by the German Embassy. Next day despite his condition he took possession of the vehicle from me as a gift from Hitler.

Many people still remember the frequent visits of King Boris of Bulgaria to Germany. I had the good fortune not only to know him personally but also to enjoy his particular esteem for me. He often invited me to visit him in Bulgaria, but unfortunately my official duties never allowed me the time to take up his invitations. Therefore I was pleased to receive the task of delivering a bullet-proof car to King Boris. On my arrival in Sofia I learned to my horror from the German Embassy that the king had suddenly become dangerously ill. He had returned feverish from a trip to the mountains, had taken a cold bath and then gone straight to a conference during which his symptoms appeared. Next morning he was unable to rise and died a few days later. I remained a week longer than planned in Sofia to attend the funeral. One month later I presented Hitler's car to Prince Regent Kyrill, the king's brother.

I could go on naming the Heads of State and leading political personalities of those years, today maligned or condemned, to whom

I brought armoured limousines. Vidkun Quisling of Norway was among them, as was the Yugoslav Head of State. I wonder what happened to the car that went to General Franco?

Chapter 3

On the Berghof

WHEN I VISITED OBERSALZBERG for the first time, at Easter 1932, it was a very awkward place to reach. After snowfall you could not drive up there, and the only recourse was to rent a sledge for the luggage and tramp uphill towing it. Because of his incapacity, a horse would be brought down for Dr Joseph Goebbels, but his wife and her son Harald had to walk up.

At that time Haus Wachenfeld on the Obersalzberg was not owned by Hitler, so he had rented it from a Frau Winter, whose husband had given it to her as a birthday gift. Wachenfeld was her maiden name. Haus Wachenfeld was not large and only a few guests could be accommodated there. If a number of acquaintances and colleagues wanted to visit Hitler they had to be put up in guesthouses or at the Platterhof hotel.

I personally delighted in the glorious Berchtesgaden landscape and the days I spent there were very restful. The household was run by Hitler's half-sister Frau Raubal. She was a good cook and knew how to make our stay pleasant.

As more and more sales of *Mein Kampf* were made in 1933, the money became available to purchase Haus Wachenfeld. Hitler himself then designed the fundamental rebuilding work to be undertaken: Haus Wachenfeld was to be expanded into the Berghof.

Obersalzberg was suddenly fashionable. Buildings went up everywhere. Hitler was not living there alone either: Bormann had sized up the situation. Hitler tended to be reclusive and loved to be alone. For this reason he had a fence put up around the property. When Bormann finished building his own house near the Berghof he attempted to convince Hitler to take down the fence, but was unsuccessful: Hitler told him that he had paid for the plot of land with his own money and he would do with it as he wanted.

In the autumn of 1936 Frau Raubal left the Berghof and soon afterwards married Professor Hamitsch, who towards the end of the war fell in action as an officer. From the departure of Frau Raubal until the outbreak of war there were several older women installed as managers or housekeepers at the Berghof. None of them could tolerate the altitude and most resigned after a brief period of employment.

After the war began, Eva Braun took over the duties as 'housewife' at the Berghof, and she was assisted by a young married couple who acted as the administrators. Long before I entered his service, Hitler had got to know Eva Braun through Heinrich Hoffmann, who employed her at his photographic studio in Munich. As the Hoffmann firm handled all photographic material relating to Hitler, Hitler spent a lot of time at the studio. Gradually a friendship developed between Hitler and the female employee, but this did not take on a more definite form until 1936.

When one of Eva Braun's female friends stayed at the Berghof for a short while it fuelled the later rumours that Eva Braun had two children by Hitler. Eva was very fond of the children of this friend, played with them and was often photographed in their company.

If circumstances allowed, my boss would spend every weekend and of course his vacations on the Obersalzberg, often going on long rambles with his guests into the mountains. If Hitler had been asked at that time what spot on the Earth's surface he considered home, I expect he would have said 'the Obersalzberg'. It became very popular within a few years. Thousands of people, curious to see

Hitler, arrived daily. After Hitler was appointed Reich Chancellor, he used the Berghof to some extent for the purposes of government: State visits and receptions were held there, kings, princes, ministers and diplomats arrived as guests. Among the most frequent visitors from abroad was King Boris of Bulgaria.

Security on the Obersalzberg was in the hands of the RSD (Reich Security Service), which was directly accountable to Heinrich Himmler. It had been created in 1933 as a special police force for the personal protection of Hitler, his ministers and foreign statesmen. It was run on straightforward police lines, and the first officers recruited had previously provided the personal security for Heinrich Held, the former Bavarian minister–president. Initially, many of them were neither SS nor NSDAP members, and some who remained in Hitler's immediate presence until the capitulation never joined the Party. For state visits, a Waffen-SS company was constantly on hand for sentry duties and in a formal capacity. They had barracks on the Obersalzberg and did a six-month tour of duty.

In 1939, life on the Obersalzberg was rural and peaceful. During the war Hitler seldom went there and instead spent his time in one or other of the Führer-HQs. Only Eva Braun remained, finally leaving the Berghof in March 1945 to end her life at Hitler's side in Berlin.

Chapter 4

Professor Dr Theodor Morell

ONE OF THE STRANGEST and most controversial personalities around Hitler was his personal physician Professor Dr Theodor Morell. One cannot speak of Hitler's entourage without taking a look at this man, even though I have no opinion on his medical skill. Since it was indisputable that he achieved certain medical successes as Hitler's personal physician, his influence was considerable.

In 1938, press photographer Hoffmann was seriously ill and his doctors had given him up as a hopeless case. Hoffmann therefore decided to invite Dr Morell down from Berlin. After a short while, Hoffmann started getting better, and a few weeks in Morell's care was sufficient for a full cure. Hitler, who was very attached to Hoffmann, felt indebted to the doctor, inviting him to visit and also accompany him as a guest on his travels. It was not long before a certain antipathy towards Dr Morell was being felt amongst the entourage, and none of us was very pleased when Hitler decided, after the annexation of Austria, to have him along as a guest on the referendum circuit. At this time Morell had no official office. However, he made life difficult for all of us. He was clumsy and slow. Once he missed the car and got left behind. Afterwards he complained to Hitler that everything was done too fast. Because the boss was very sensitive about hospitality to his guests, and always placed special value on their feeling happy, Morell caused us all a great deal of annoyance. He took no interest in us at all and was soon the least favourite of the guests.

One referendum meeting in Austria followed another. Finally we came to Innsbruck. Since there was no hall, the people who had come from all over the Tyrol in great numbers had to be found tents. At the conclusion of the event these people were not ready to retire, and despite the foggy, damp weather Hitler felt obliged to make repeated appearances on the broad balcony of his hotel from his warm room. That evening it was obvious that he had caught a chill.

Travelling physician Dr Karl Brandt was called to make a diagnosis and announced after a thorough examination: 'Mein Führer, for you the campaign is over. Tomorrow you will be hoarse and unable to speak.' Hitler was up in arms. 'Impossible. I cannot go home in the middle of a campaign. Impossible, Brandt!'

Morell heard about the sudden indisposition and had himself summoned. He asked to see the throat, then stated shortly: 'If you follow my instructions, mein Führer, you will be well again tomorrow.' Morell was economic with words. Hitler had to go to bed at once and received from Morell a vitamin injection. He had to inhale all night through a device from the pharmacy and additionally keep applying hot oil compresses. Next morning the chill was gone, and Hitler was able to deliver his speech in the evening.

After returning to Berlin, Hitler suggested to Morell that he should join his personal service as a specialist in internal medicine. Morell accepted and transferred his private practice in Berlin to a representative. From now on he belonged in the most intimate circle around Hitler and accompanied us on virtually all our journeys.

There is no doubt that Morell as a doctor was pleasant and friendly. He was ready to attend whenever called. He made no exceptions, and it was irrelevant to him if his patient were an officer or a simple soldier. In that manner over the course of time he built up a large circle of friends amongst the intermediate and lower ranks. He had no real relationships with the higher-ups. It was his basic philosophy that he was a doctor and nothing but a doctor. He did not want social links.

Unlike Hitler, Morell was a hearty eater and it was impossible to prepare a table too rich for him. This made him the butt of many jokes, and he was often ridiculed for it. Morell took no notice and dismissed all criticism with the observation that the important thing was how it all tasted. Eating was actually his one great pleasure in life. He neither smoke nor drank and probably had a low opinion of women. Morell's great success was his vitamin treatments. He made up the vitamins for injection or as tablets, almost all of the preparations being made in his own pharmaceutical laboratory in Hamburg.

He often had surprising successes. Karl Krause, who was one of Hitler's personal servants from July 1934 to September 1939, fell ill with double pneumonia about ten days before a planned visit to Italy. Morell took over his treatment. After eight days Krause was well enough to resume his duties and make the trip.

While studying in Germany, Lady Unity Mitford, a sister-in-law of Oswald Mosley, was invited to be Hitler's guest at the Bayreuth Festival. During the Festival she fell ill with double pneumonia and pleurisy. When Hitler heard of this he sent Morell to treat her. In this case Morell was again able to cure the patient within a few days.

During my internment post war I frequently came across Morell in the various camps. There were rumours circulating about him, and for this reason I discussed with him why he had been dismissed by Hitler. Serious accusations had been levelled against him by the press, radio and the medical profession. He was very depressed about it and insisted repeatedly that he had never given Hitler overdoses of medication. He had always done his best to fortify Hitler only by the use of vitamin preparations and glucose. This could not be avoided because of Hitler's unbalanced diet. Hitler had understood that. On my enquiry as to how the rumours had started that Morell systematically poisoned Hitler during his treatment of him at the behest of a foreign power, he provided the following explanation:

As the result of the assassination attempt of 20 July 1944, Hitler had been suffering from ear damage. One day the ENT (ear, nose and throat) specialist was waiting in Hitler's bedroom as Hitler was indisposed. Out of curiosity he looked at some objects on the table and noticed a small box labelled 'Anti-Gas Tablets'. Below the heading the prescription stated that three to four had to be taken daily before meals. As we now know, one of the compound ingredients of these tablets was strychnine. Where they came from I still do not know, but in any case Hitler was taking them long before I took over his treatment. On the occasions when I asked him about them he told me that he took them only sporadically if he had really bad stomach trouble. As his personal physician I saw no reason to object to their use.

The ENT specialist took away a sample of the tablets for laboratory analysis, and no doubt the tests confirmed the presence of strychnine in them. Professor Dr Brandt, who had taken over as Reich Commissioner for Health after leaving the post of travelling physician, was staying at FHQ (Führer-HQ) at the time. This specialist saw it as his duty to report the matter to Brandt. The latter, who was very jealous of me, as a result of which there was a very tense atmosphere between us, now saw his chance to bring about my downfall. He contacted the duty manservant Arndt at once: 'Tell me, Arndt, the Führer keeps some anti-gas tablets in his bedroom. How many does he actually take each day?' Arndt answered correctly: 'It varies. It depends on whether he has flatulence or not.' This answer did not satisfy Brandt. 'By God I am going to find out how many he takes each day!' Intimidated, Arndt said: 'It might be that he takes twenty.' 'So, twenty tablets daily,

Arndt!' and without further ado Brandt hung up. Brandt therefore created a totally false impression, for Hitler did not take the tablets daily; they were there just for when he had intestinal problems.

After the telephone conversation, Brandt held a conference with the ENT specialist and duty surgeon Dr Hans Karl von Hasselbach. These gentlemen, none of them a specialist in internal medicine, reckoned that by taking twenty tablets daily Hitler would have a high level of strychnine in his body. They also calculated the amount he would have taken since I took office with him in 1938. Since, as is known, strychnine is not expelled by the body and is stored, the three doctors believed they would soon have the proof that I had been systematically poisoning Hitler. Brandt now reported this 'discovery' to Himmler who came to FHQ post haste to start the investigation himself.

That day,* as I was entering the dining room for lunch, Brandt asked me: 'Tell me, Morell, you have been treating the Führer for some years now. Do you actually know what is wrong with him?' I answered: 'Of course. Hitler is healthy except for occasional severe flatulence. He also suffers from vitamin deficiency, which I treat with injections of vitamins and glucose.'

'No, Herr Morell, you are mistaken!' Brandt replied brusquely, 'over the years you have been systematically poisoning the Führer. Once we have made a precise investigation we shall know what is truly wrong with him.' I had not expected that. Deeply distressed and depressed I hurried to Hitler and informed him of their suspicions. He calmed me and said he would look into it. As I was leaving the Führer-bunker, Himmler came up to me fuming: 'You – if you have been poisoning the Führer, then you've had it! Believe me, I'll have you strung up at once!'

At that moment Hitler, who had probably heard Himmler's threat, appeared and told the Reichsführer-SS that I was the only

---

* According to the other sources these events transpired on 7 October 1944.

doctor who had given him proper treatment. 'And as for the tablets that is my personal business. And you, Herr Himmler, are not to poke your nose into affairs that do not concern you.' As Hitler's ear injury had healed, the ENT specialist had to leave FHQ at once.* The duty surgeon von Hasselbach† was transferred to the front. Brandt was expelled from FHQ with orders never to return unless told to do so in the course of his duty.'‡

This conversation with Morell has remained almost verbatim in my memory. After being discharged from Allied internment, he died in the most impoverished circumstances at Rottach am Tegernsee on 28 May 1948 after an illness.

---

* The ENT specialist was Dr Erwin Giesing. He returned to a Hamburg hospital.

† Dr SS-Hauptsturmführer Karl von Hasselbach served on the Western Front in a military field hospital from 8 October 1944 until the capitulation.

‡ Dr SS-Gruppenführer Karl Brandt, from 1942 Commissioner-General for Health and Hygiene, was arrested in April 1945 for defeatism and sentenced to death. Having survived the war he was arrested by the Allies, tried for crimes against humanity (euthanasia programme and experiments on concentration camp inmates) and sentenced to death. He was hanged at Landsberg Prison on 2 June 1948.

Chapter 5

Martin Bormann

THE MOST HATED AND dictatorial person in Hitler's immediate circle was Reichsleiter Martin Bormann. He had a cat-like, effusive show of friendliness when it suited his purposes, but when not being nice he was utterly brutal. His ruthlessness knew no bounds. His only known good point was his unbelievable work rate. One cannot talk about the fall of the Reich and the death of Hitler without a thorough understanding of the person who was the grey eminence in Hitler's personal circle.

I got to know Bormann in Munich in 1932. At that time he was relatively unknown until his appointment as head of the SA (Sturmabteilung) in-house insurance organisation, later that year. He had an excellent idea of how to make equals feel he was their friend and to have himself appreciated by his superiors. He worked almost day and night without a break and rightfully won the reputation of being a great workhorse. When Rudolf Hess was expanding the liaison apparatus between Party and State he noticed Bormann and took him into the staff. After a short while Bormann rose to be Stabsleiter (head of staff) under Hess and had thus achieved his first goal. He belonged in the first team. He remained pleasant and was always ready to be of service to equals and those above him.

Things changed in 1936. After Hitler's Haus Wachenfeld on the Obersalzberg was rebuilt and expanded into the Berghof, Bormann burst out from his previously modest disguise. Now he just had to have a house on the Obersalzberg. This would give him a reason for being constantly in close proximity to Hitler, with whom he would otherwise have little to do in the course of his duties. In general, his only appearances at the Berghof were to accompany Hess there and stand by silently while Hess delivered his oral reports to Hitler.

Bormann therefore started to buy up land on the Obersalzberg. The so-called reason for this was that it was being done on behalf of Rudolf Hess to create for Hitler a place where he could really find peace and recuperate without disturbance. To assist in this enterprise he founded an NSDAP financial consortium. He bought up tracts of land from local farmers. There was no need for him to use underhand methods for the purpose, for he had made it known that the NSDAP would pay four to five times over the market value. This speculation in land could not be kept secret from Hitler for ever. He was concerned that Bormann might be using intimidation to force people off their property, and so told the adjutancy to warn Bormann that at the first complaint he would put a stop to it. Bormann assured him that there were no grounds for disquiet: on the contrary, the farmers were actually coming to him offering to sell. Once Hitler's mind was set at rest, Bormann's buying spree on behalf of the NSDAP knew no bounds. Soon he had acquired the whole Obersalzberg mountain.

The time now seemed ripe for Bormann to spin his web around Hitler even tighter. At that time, it was the practice at the Berghof for the duty adjutant to decide which Party leaders and men from the State and Wehrmacht to invite to lunch with Hitler. One day Bormann contacted the adjutant with a request to be invited to dine, should the Führer approve. Obviously Bormann was approved. Shortly before the meal he telephoned the duty adjutant again to excuse himself from attending because his workload was too great. This happened several times. When he finally appeared for lunch one day he was late and took the opportunity to apologise to Hitler with the explanation that he was so weighed down with work that it had unfortunately not been possible for him to get away on time. He kept this ploy going so long that slowly but surely Hitler gained the impression that Bormann was the most industrious man in the whole Party apparatus.

After winning Hitler's trust in this way, Bormann was given the stewardship of the Berghof. Thus he achieved another goal and won a fresh position of power from where he could damage his rivals. The expansion of his jurisdiction allowed Bormann to be nastier in his relationship towards subordinates. He began to feel secure. To his underlings he became the most irrational superior. One moment he would treat them in the kindest and most pleasant manner, even giving out presents, and a few minutes later he would be a sadist – belittling, offensive and wounding. Often he would go into such a rage that one would think he had lost his reason.

Once the entire staff was under his control, Bormann was empowered to hire and fire whomsoever he wanted. Woe betide the subordinate who fell into disfavour with him. He would persecute that person, filled with hate, for so long as he remained within reach. His behaviour was totally different to those people whom he knew Hitler liked and did not stand in his path. Towards them his friendship was unlimited and he would bend over backwards to make sure Hitler noticed.

Bormann's great passion was building. It was his method to sketch all the fancy ideas that he knew he shared with Hitler. Thus on the Obersalzberg he converted the houses that appeared to him appropriate for the purpose, making them into guest houses and small villas while creating for himself the wonderful opportunity to go over the plans with Hitler and so ingratiate himself with him even more.

Hitler loved the Dietrich Eckhardt Room at the Platterhof hotel especially because it was tied to many memories for him. Bormann had the whole building – except for this one room – pulled down, and rebuilt a new Platterhof around it. This kind of thing was naturally very pleasing to Hitler. Additionally, Bormann carried out every order he received from Hitler absolutely reliably and in the quickest possible time.

One day Bormann had the idea of building something extraordinary for the Führer. It was an absurd structure and cost a fortune. He put a tea house on the highest peak of the 1,800-metre high Kehlstein. He had a road laid, which led to within 100 metres of the peak. Then he put a vertical shaft through the rock so that the tea house was accessible only by this one lift. Hitler, however, placed no great value on the Bormann tea house project, although later he liked to take guests there.

In the autumn of 1940, the Italian crown princess Marie José, sister of the king of Belgium, was Hitler's guest on the Kehlstein. Arthur Kannenberg, the house catering manager at the Reich Chancellery in Berlin, was called down from the capital to handle the arrangements, and was responsible for ensuring that the reception went off smoothly. Unfortunately the tea was served boiling hot and the princess burned her mouth. Hitler was terribly put out and apologised repeatedly. Although the royal guest dismissed the incident in a joking manner, there were recriminations once she had gone. Kannenberg blamed the adjutant, Brückner, who had relieved him of supervision of the manservants.

In order to get to the bottom of it, Hitler asked Bormann to investigate. This was grist to Bormann's mill. It had long been his aim to get rid of Brückner, and for years he had been compiling a dossier on him. Now the time had come to put his plans into effect. He argued that, at fifty-six years old, Brückner was too old to hold down such a demanding position as chief adjutant. The Führer should pension him off. As it happened, Brückner would have been happy to have accepted such a proposal if it had been tied to an honourable retirement. A younger and more versatile successor should have no problem in mastering the job. Hitler asked Bormann for further evidence of Brückner's unsuitability. When Bormann supplied it, Hitler declined to read the material but allowed himself to be convinced of the need to retire Brückner on the grounds of age. The parting was apparently on the friendliest terms.

Bormann now began the big clear-out in the Personal Adjutancy. He got rid of everybody he did not like, it being immaterial how good, reliable or capable they might be at their job, and he replaced them with people who would kowtow to him. After Brückner's departure Julius Schaub took over the job of chief adjutant and head of the Personal Adjutancy, but he was no more than a figurehead. Bormann was the driving force behind everything. With the keys of the castle in his hands he could intrigue against all and sundry, and in pursuit of influence on Hitler he spared no effort to remove people who would not obey him blindly. If he could not find some breach of discipline against them and they would not go voluntarily he would arrange for his 'friend' Himmler to employ the person temporarily at a miserable wage.

Between Bormann and Himmler there seemed to be an extraordinarily genial relationship. Outwardly they were the best of friends. When they met they poured praises on each other. Instead of offering the right hand they would clasp both hands jovially. Actually they were arch-enemies and hated each other. Each envied the other for his influence on Hitler, and were empire-building.

My own relationship with Martin Bormann was tense, from the beginning of his influence until the end of the Reich. He always had some plan afoot to get Hitler to dismiss me. He failed because I had Hitler's trust. Through my constant personal contact with Hitler I always had the opportunity to put my case in rebuttal of Bormann's insinuations. Bormann knew how low an opinion I had of him.

It was of special satisfaction to Bormann to receive the news at the Berghof in May 1941 of Rudolf Hess's flight to Britain. Hess's adjutant brought Hitler a letter in which Hess announced his flight and provided his reasons for making it. He would attempt to negotiate the basis for a special peace with Britain. Hess, who knew Hitler's pro-British leanings, believed he could render great service to the German people by his mission, and thereby save the world great unhappiness. Hitler himself, who had been frustrated in all his attempts to reach an accord with Great Britain, was convinced immediately that Hess's effort was doomed to failure. Beyond a doubt he had no prior knowledge of his deputy's intentions.

The flight to Britain came as a tremendous surprise to us all. Hitler quickly concluded that Hess had acted while the balance of his mind was disturbed. His adjutant on the other hand believed himself to be the bearer of good tidings, and was thus astonished to be arrested. Orders were given immediately that all members of Hess's personal staff were to be held as accomplices. Later interrogations revealed that Hess had undertaken his mission on the advice of an astrologer. Thereafter Hitler spoke only seldom of his former deputy. If the subject of Hess was even mentioned, he would emphasise strongly that the flight had been made from the best ideals and intentions. There was no question of any kind of treachery.

Bormann now succeeded Hess. Having precise knowledge about his former staff he advised Hitler on all those questions where previously Hess had had jurisdiction. The name of Hess's office – the Liaison Staff – was replaced by 'The Party Chancellery'. Here again Bormann began with his customary cleansing operation. He was now controlling an office from where he could meddle in the affairs of Party and State and so maximise his power structure. His first duty as he saw it was to erase anything that recalled Hess. He ordered all pictures of him to be taken down and forbade any discussion about the flight to Britain. Books and official Party publications in which an image of Hess appeared, and even school books that mentioned the Führer's deputy were confiscated and destroyed. His almost manic hate for Hess resulted in him changing the forename of his son Rudolf, named for his godfather Rudolf Hess, and appointing new godparents.

Bormann's tyranny embraced his whole family. Though unimportant when seen against the great events of the time, it seems to me pertinent to an understanding of Bormann's personality to quote an example of his behaviour from his private life. Gruppenführer Fegelein married sometime in May 1944.* The reception was held at Bormann's residence on the Obersalzberg. At about two in the morning Bormann suddenly decided he should wear a smoking jacket. He asked for a particular shirt to go with it, which he had worn a few days before. Frau Bormann replied that it was in the wash. Martin Bormann erupted into a screaming fit and let his wife know that he would wear only this and no other shirt. As a punishment the wife was sent away from Obersalzberg immediately with the children and was forbidden to return unless she had his permission. Five weeks later he considered that she had atoned her guilt and he was magnanimous enough to allow her and the children to return from Munich.

Now nobody dared oppose Bormann. Even Reichsleiters and Gauleiters feared him. His father-in-law Reichsleiter Walter Buch would leave Obersalzberg in his car in a near panic if he heard that Bormann was coming up. If Hitler asked a Reichsleiter or Gauleiter personally about morale or the circumstances around them, he or she either gave the most glowing report possible or only as many of the disagreeable facts as they had rehearsed with Bormann beforehand. What they told Hitler was naturally what he had learned from Bormann himself earlier.

If at all possible, Bormann would prevent his own subordinates from going in to see Hitler face to face. Everybody, even the

---

* This was actually on 3 June. (TN)

ministers, had to obtain Bormann's consent to speak to Hitler, and he would refuse permission on the flimsiest grounds. If he could not prevent a visitor going in, he would be present in the room and attempt to steer the conversation in the direction he wanted. Reich economics minister Walter Funk once said to me: 'You cannot imagine, Erich, how incredibly difficult it has become nowadays to have a quiet talk with the Führer. Always this Bormann sticking his nose in. He finishes sentences for you, interrupts and makes any serious discussion impossible!'

For somebody who was not there, even today it is scarcely possible to conceive how this man was able to make himself so highly regarded by Hitler. Because Hitler was vegetarian, Bormann had to be so too. He would inform everybody how delicious he found the various vegetarian dishes and how they helped him enjoy his work more. When nobody was looking he would tuck into cutlets and steaks and would certainly not turn his nose up at a smoked sausage. Nobody dared let Hitler know.

Because Hitler was a non-smoker, Bormann gave it up. In fairness one must say that he succeeded, although it was a struggle. Bormann obviously knew that Hitler was an avid reader, so he employed a team of professional readers whose job it was to obtain all new publications in the literary domain and provide a succinct summary of the contents of each book. Typed up on one side of a sheet it would give Bormann enough understanding for his purpose. If he dined with Hitler in the evening, or we all ate together, he would then create for himself the opportunity to hold forth on his literary knowledge, and might say, for example: 'Mein Führer, a new book has come out about Ulrich von Hutten. It has inspired me. You really must read it.' Hitler would thus infer that Bormann must have read the book himself. He was amazed how this man, despite his enormous workload, could still find the time to read so many books. This all helped to deepen and confirm the impression that in Bormann he had a person of universal genius as a colleague.

Only towards Eva Braun was Bormann forced to keep his distance. She was the unknown factor in his calculations. Open warfare against her was not possible, although in keeping with his nature he created as many difficulties for her behind her back as he could contrive. Even today many people find it incomprehensible that Hitler allowed this man to climb all over him and the Reich, and criticise him for it. We who spent many years in close proximity to this diabolical personality all hated him. Nevertheless, to give the devil his due, he had that kind of genius for work rarely seen on the planet. He would master anything mechanical. He succeeded in making himself indispensable to Hitler, who was without doubt an intelligent man, for when Hitler gave Bormann an order he knew that of all his devoted servants only Bormann would guarantee to carry it out unconditionally, despite all adverse circumstances, and in the shortest possible time.

Here is a small example of how Bormann knew the way to arouse Hitler's admiration. On a summer's afternoon in 1938 at the Berghof, we were ready to go for a drive. Hitler gazed over the mountain scenery and observed to Bormann that he always found the panorama glorious but it was such a shame that the little old farmhouse on the slope below his property was so ugly! As soon as the old peasants, who had guaranteed occupancy until death, had passed on, the house should be pulled down.

When we returned from Munich twenty-four hours later, Hitler and I could scarcely believe our eyes. Where only yesterday we had seen the ugly little farmhouse, today there was only a meadow where red poll cattle grazed. What could have happened? As soon as the car bearing myself and Hitler had disappeared from view the previous day, Bormann had arranged with the old couple to give up the property voluntarily. He had found them a new house and they were apparently very happy to be able to please Hitler. While busy clearing out their possessions, a great army of workers was shipped in and in twenty-four hours the farmhouse had vanished as though it had never been.

A second example proves how attentive Bormann was to hear any of Hitler's ideas. As is known, thousands of people used to make their way past the Berghof when Hitler was in residence in the hope of seeing him. He would often stand for hours in the open while people drove by. One hot summer's evening he mentioned to Bormann that he found it too much of a strain, principally because he did not feel well if he spent too long in the sun. When Hitler emerged from the Berghof next day at the usual hour in order to greet the crowd waiting to see him, he was speechless to see, at the very spot where he was accustomed to stand, an enormous tree, its trunk thicker than a man, and whose leafy branches created full shade against the rays of the sun. The previous night Bormann had had it transported up to the Berg and planted there. The tree obviously liked the spot and remains there to this very day. As soon as Hitler was away, Bormann subjected the roots to an intense period of watering to ensure they took properly.

Can Hitler be blamed for being impressed by all this? Martin Bormann is dead. His influence on Hitler is probably the saddest chapter in the history of the Reich. If one speaks of Hitler's demise, one cannot overlook Bormann. Without doubt he bore a great responsibility for the overall development that found its tragic end on 30 April 1945 at the Reich Chancellery in Berlin.

Chapter 6

Signs of Disquiet

HITLER MOVED FROM ONE foreign policy success to the next. By the end of 1938, the Saar, Austria and the Sudetenland had already been incorporated into the Reich. Hitler was in the best of spirits and felt stronger and more secure than ever.

On the morning of 15 March 1939 I received the order to send a convoy of vehicles including cross-country cars to Dresden and remain in constant contact with it. However, Czech President Hácha was expected in Berlin, so I drove the CD limousine to the Anhalter railway station to fetch him. As I manoeuvred into the courtyard of the New Reich Chancellery, the Czech national anthem rang out. Hácha inspected the guard of honour of the *SS-Leibstandarte* and was greeted by Hitler at the entrance of the Chancellery. The negotiations lasted into the morning of 16 March. I heard that Hácha had collapsed under the nervous strain, so Dr Morell was sent for to fortify the Czech leader with injections of vitamins and glucose. Early that morning the first treaties were settled. One of my drivers took Hácha back to the station for his train to Prague.

Meanwhile, on my instructions, my convoy – ten cross-country vehicles and cars, and four trucks – had proceeded to a small railway station on the Saxon–Czech border. Towards 0630 hrs Hitler left Berlin with the entourage in the Führer-train, and alighted at the Czech border, where my convoy of vehicles awaited, in a blizzard. I took my place at the wheel of the Führer's cross-country automobile. Hitler sat beside me and we led off the convoy.

The customs officers at both frontiers appeared to have orders to allow us to pass. No attempt was made to stop us and the barriers were raised at our approach. The blizzard grew fiercer. We drove across Czechoslovakia at slow speed. The highways were slippery and one of our trucks went into a ditch. Its load was transferred at once to the other vehicles, and the truck was abandoned. We had no time to waste. Prague was reached at four that afternoon. Life in the venerable old city was going on as normal. Our passage through the streets went almost unnoticed. The snow storm continued.

At the Hradčany Castle, seat of the Czech government, we were not expected, but quarters were arranged for us in a wing of the castle. A single company from an SS engineer battalion arrived, the remainder having been held up by the blizzard and icy roads. Towards 1700 hrs President Hácha, arriving by train from Berlin, came to the castle. He was astonished to see Hitler there waiting for him. He had not thought it possible for him to act so swiftly. The talks were resumed at once, treaties drafted and signed. Next day the Czech Cabinet and a few military commanders arrived at the Hradčany. They were received and presented to Hitler.

This military occupation of Prague had been effected by an invasion force consisting of Hitler, his military escort and one company of an SS engineer battalion. This battalion had been formed in Dresden from a training unit under instruction and was so poorly armed that the men of the Führer's SS bodyguard had to lend them half their stock of machine pistols. Looking back on this situation today, it would have been no problem for the Czechs to have captured the lot of us. We had no heavy weapons and could have held out for only a few minutes.

On the afternoon of 17 March our convoy of vehicles left Prague. Heading north we passed the German occupation force heading for the Czech capital. At our original departure point on the frontier we boarded the special train for Vienna, where Hitler was expected.

*

Everybody has his good and bad side. Hitler made mistakes, but when he is accused today of lacking personal courage that is unfounded. His entourage, led by Bormann and the generals, often criticised him for being too audacious for a Head of State: every day, for example, I drove Hitler myself to the frontline to watch manoeuvres during the Polish campaign. Most of all I shall never forget a flight to Zaporozhye on the Dnieper, during the winter of 1942. The Russians were making a huge push to recapture the Donetz Basin – their main objective being the giant power station at Zaporozhye. We touched down at the western airport, the Russians having already seized back the eastern one with their tank spearhead. The generals begged Hitler in vain to get out of Zaporozhye, but he wanted to obtain a first-hand impression of the situation and so declined to leave. Not until the western airport came under attack from Rata fighters and he was satisfied that he had been sufficiently well informed during his four-day stay, and had ordered the necessary countermeasures, did Hitler give the order to leave. From Zaporozhye we flew to Vinniza near Zhitomir in the Ukraine, the summer FHQ on the Eastern Front, from where he proposed to visit endangered sectors of the front as and when problems arose.

Nothing could be further from my mind than to glorify Hitler. When people from the Hitler period feel justified in making the allegation today in their so-called memoirs that Hitler always avoided visiting the front in order to keep himself out of harm's way, that is a lie. The generals kept telling him that the conduct of the war would suffer if he absented himself from FHQ for long periods, and he allowed himself to be convinced. If danger materialised at critical spots, and he believed his personal attendance was required, he threw caution to the winds.

Neither is it the purpose of my book to portray how Hitler influenced the fighting. It is not something for which I feel competent. It must be the task of future historians to separate fact from fiction. Apart from my few journeys home and abroad on official duty, I spent virtually the entire war within the closest circle at FHQ. Life there was simple, and involved working from morning till night. Actually Hitler insisted repeatedly that all members of his staff should spend time with an active unit for so-called 'proven at the front' status, but I was one of the few exceptions. Despite volunteering on a number of occasions I was never given approval to go. Hitler told me that I was indispensable even for short periods.

Without any doubt the decisive influence on war policy came from Field Marshal Wilhelm Keitel, Colonel General Alfred Jodl and whoever happened to be chief of the army general staff at the time. Despite Bormann's personal influence on Hitler he did not take part in the daily military situation conferences until January 1945. Even Himmler had not been justified in attending initially, but was eventually accepted as time went on as leader of the Waffen-SS.

When Hitler moved into the Führer-bunker in Berlin in 1945, as the last phase of the war began, Martin Bormann achieved his last goal. He was present at nearly every military situation conference[*] and was certainly amongst those who continued to exercise that influence on Hitler which convinced him to keep fighting to the last man.

---

[*] In his capacity as head of the Volkssturm. (TN)

Chapter 7

In the Führer-bunker in Berlin

S TILL IN MOURNING I returned in January 1945 from my
father's funeral at Oberhausen. At FHQ Ziegenberg near
Bad Nauheim everything had changed for the worse.
Burdened by troubles and worry, we knew that a hard, difficult time
had begun for all Germany. The casualty lists grew longer every
day. Overwhelmed, our troops were flooding back. Even using
our last elite divisions at Malmedy had not brought the expected
success. On all fronts the enemy was meeting only light resistance.
The heaviest air raids by the American and British air fleets were
reducing our cities to rubble. Endlessly, by day and night, squadron
after squadron bombed our cities, our women and children. Our
armaments production was impaired and hit hard; our ability to
supply troops at the front with weapons and ammunition called
into question. The gravity of the situation affected our morale. 'The
FHQ has been transferred to Berlin!' Hearing these words on my
arrival at Ziegenberg came as a shock. What could be the reason?

When we of the entourage occasionally discussed a possible
decisive battle for Germany we had assumed that Hitler would
direct it from southern Germany, since all technical preparations for
it had already been put in place there. I was therefore very surprised
that the final phase of this war was to be directed from Berlin. I met
the clearing unit and some staff officers at Ziegenberg. Telexes with
the latest instructions were being distributed, couriers came and
went with files and other materials, while heavily laden trucks left

Ziegenberg for the Reich capital. I found out that Hitler had not left for Berlin until late in the afternoon. Accompanied by his personal staff, he had left Friedberg in Upper Hessen in his special train.

Still strongly affected by the stresses of the last few days I took the car and sped through the night for the capital. A telex had already reached the Reich Chancellery driver pool advising of the Führer's imminent arrival. When I arrived I found all my vehicles ready to go. When the Führer-train rolled into Berlin-Grunewald at six on the dot that morning I was already waiting at the station with my convoy. Despite my own tensions I was shocked to see how Hitler looked. From his face you could tell how much the journey had tired him. His special train was equipped with all the latest innovations in telecommunications so that he could be kept continuously informed of events during long train journeys, and then transmit his orders to the relevant military centres. At Berlin-Grunewald that morning he had concluded the last train journey of his life.

Before Hitler went to bed, his manservant summoned me to the Führer's presence. I was very touched at the way he enquired about the sudden death of my father, despite his own much more pressing problems. He made me recount everything, then offered me both his hands to express his sympathy. For the first time I noticed that the war had not left him unmarked, and that he had grown old.

In the rooms of the Reich Chancellery an excited activity reigned. Nobody had prepared for our arrival. Hitler's decision must have been taken on the spur of the moment and against the advice of Bormann and his own military leaders. Parts of the Old Reich Chancellery had already been demolished by heavy bombing. Bearing in mind the heavier air raids to be expected in future, the cellar rooms, which had been expanded into bunkers, were occupied as soon as possible by the military centres attached to FHQ, while the remainder, especially the Wehrmacht command staff and OKH

(Army High Command), had gone directly from Ziegenberg to Zossen-Jüterbog fifty kilometres south of Berlin.

Separating the FHQ and Wehrmacht staffs, relocating them in two geographically distant areas, gave rise to an extraordinarily difficult situation for which we were in no way prepared. New telephone lines had to be laid to guarantee faultless telecommunications. The signals apparatus hummed ceaselessly, and orders echoed through the subterranean passageways of the Reich Chancellery.

The division of the available rooms caused us much difficulty. Everything had to be reorganised. Suitable accommodation for Hitler's female secretaries had to be found. Since the departure of General Halder several years previously, every order given and word spoken in the military situation conferences had been recorded by former Reichstag stenographers. Hitler's intention was to rebut by the true record all counterarguments challenging what he had said. This gave rise within a short while to great mountains of files containing the transcripts. My own duties now included maintaining contact with Zossen-Jüterbog and other military centres by vehicle, insofar as that remained possible.

Stalin's divisions stood at the gates of Berlin. Our positions were holding despite the most determined enemy assaults. For the time being the enemy had relaxed the pressure. The lull before the storm . . . Large troop formations and tank units of the Red Army waited a few kilometres away, pending orders to attack. The last great offensive was imminent. Would we be able to stop the enemy – or would they annihilate us? Our duties, every day more arduous, made the greatest demands of officers and men. My own men drove day and night. Regular hours for sleep were abandoned. Generals and other officers of Hitler's personal staff had to be driven to and from front sectors and command posts by the quickest routes.

We had the most extraordinary luck. We never lost a vehicle or a passenger en route.

As it was impossible to get out and about, we doubled as civil defence men, assisted the fire brigades during bombing raids and lent a hand in the ways soldiers are bound to do in such desperate situations. I never heard a word of complaint from any of my men. Each knew how grave things were. Additionally we laboured under great mental pressure because of the ever-worsening reports from every front. Even in the West our troops were pulling back. Our best units could not survive the heavy air attacks, the effects of which were too great for entrenched positions to be held.

Field Marshal Albert Kesselring was appointed Commander-in-Chief West in March 1945. We had lost Italy. Our former FHQ at Ziegenberg was now Kesselring's HQ. He came to Berlin frequently in order to deliver precise oral reports about the front and the general situation. Worried about the safety of Kesselring, of whose military qualities he had the highest opinion, Hitler asked me to name somebody on whom I could rely absolutely to get the C-in-C safely to Bad Nauheim. Insofar as such a guarantee was possible to give, I had to nominate myself, and thus I placed myself personally at Kesselring's disposal.

At that time ever greater demands were being made of me. In my BMW I made frightening drives day and night between Berlin and Ziegenberg. They were the most hair-raising journeys I ever made. Bomb craters gaped along the smooth surface of the autobahns, and vehicles shot to pieces and burnt out after low-level air attacks were piled up to make barricades.

On 15 or 16 March 1945 (I cannot be certain which) Hitler announced unexpectedly that he intended to visit the frontline. The close circle objected to this idea more vehemently than on previous occasions. Bormann and the generals got together to talk him out of it, but he would not be dissuaded. His idea was to see the frontline for himself, look at troop strengths and the ammunition situation. Around noon we left Berlin for Frankfurt an der Oder. Whenever we were recognised, people thronged around the car. The personal presence of Hitler gave them new hope in a predicament that we already saw as hopeless.

Hitler spoke with officers and other ranks, women and children. The magic of his great personality radiated from him. Often with a few words he succeeded in putting fresh heart into those in despair. On the drive back he sat next to me sunk in thought, the gravity of the situation casting its shadow over his features. He did not speak. This was to be the last time he sat beside me in a car. From now until his death he spent every day and night in his bunker.

Once safely back in Berlin, my only wish was for sleep, to recover from the strenuous efforts to which I had been subjected that week. Scarcely had my head hit the pillow than a manservant asked me to report to Hitler. After enquiring after my health he asked whether I felt fit enough to accompany Minister Speer on a visit to the front. He probably knew how much I had done over recent days but wanted to entrust Speer to me since he was not satisfied that Speer's own driver was up to it.

It was Speer's birthday, 19 March. Shortly before leaving for the front with Speer, I joined with other well-wishers in a small celebration at his office. Although we were all trying to forget our problems and worries for a few hours there was precious little cheer to be found.

Towards two in the morning we headed out of Berlin in two vehicles. On reaching the Western Front I camouflaged the car by painting it with mud. We drove on. The conditions were very bad. There was little conversation. During the night I drove the car without lights through columns of vehicles and wrecks. Speer and his escort spent most of the time asleep. We went from one command post to the next. At each the commanders had to supply endless information. How many weapons do you still have? How much ammunition? How many vehicles . . . what troops? Speer required an accurate answer to each question. The tour of inspection lasted five days. We came under persistent attack by low-level aircraft. Bombs exploded to the right and left of my vehicle, which remained miraculously undamaged. Whenever this happened, Speer and the rest of us would jump clear like scared rabbits. 'Brakes on! Out of the car! Nose into the mud of a wayside ditch! A careful look at the sky. Looks like they are leaving.' Seeking cover from place to place we then edged back to the vehicle, and I put my foot down on the accelerator – until we were attacked again.

On the evening of my return to Berlin I went to the lobby in front of the situation room. In these rooms of the Führer-bunker the destiny of Germany was decided. From here, millions of soldiers received their orders. Telex operators and telephonists worked in shifts around the clock, day and night. Officers came for their orders and went. Despite the enormous concentration of activity here, an almost sepulchral quiet reigned in this brain centre of the Reich. Hitler was in a situation conference, so I waited in the lobby. Many old acquaintances passed by, enquiring after my wellbeing in a soft whisper. Everybody had news to give. Naturally I was asked how things looked in the West.

When the situation conference ended, Hitler emerged with his advisers. I stood up immediately to report my return from the front. Minister Speer who had attended the conference probably told him of the success of our excursion. As soon as Hitler saw me he left his entourage, in that spontaneous way he had, hugged me like a lost son and shook both my hands warmly. He thanked me repeatedly for bringing Speer back safely. Bormann stood at the rear of the group with a savage expression on his face. He was rubbing his knuckles nervously as was his custom when something annoyed him. As I discovered later, during my absence he had made a fresh attempt to interest Hitler in replacing me with a personal driver and companion more acceptable to Bormann. I knew that for a year he had been grooming a man he wanted to present to Hitler as soon as he had managed to topple me. There was no mean trick to which he would not stoop to prise me away from Hitler. I was the last of the Old Faithfuls with his own office, somebody who without the need for an order or invitation from Hitler could visit him personally in his private or service rooms. This fact alone was enough to make me hated in Bormann's eyes.

Since this enmity from within Hitler's immediate circle was most unpleasant, I had made regular requests to be transferred to the front. Hitler always turned these down. One day when I firmly repeated my request – I was especially distressed by Bormann's attitude – Hitler told me: 'You have a greater responsibility here than at the front. Moreover my life, which I have entrusted to you so often, is more important to me than this constant sniping by Herr Bormann.'

Weeks of high tension passed. Endless bomber formations over-flew those territories of the Reich as yet unconquered. Marshal Zhukov was still building up ever larger numbers of troops at the gates of Berlin, but he was short of what he needed for the decisive blow.

On the Führer's fifty-sixth birthday, 20 April 1945, I reflected on past years when the German people celebrated this day, and held great receptions and parades. When first employed in 1932 I dreamed of being his chauffeur and constant companion on the road, to have a modest place in his attempts for peaceful solutions to the problems we faced. Within limits, life fulfilled my wish. However, 20 April 1945 was a different birthday to all the rest. Around the walls of the Reich capital the armies of his greatest enemy threatened. There were no festivities or parades, although in the bunker at least there reigned a more lively atmosphere than in recent days. Shortly before midnight on 19 April the military and personal staffs arrived to offer their congratulations: Field Marshal

Keitel, Colonel General Jodl and General Burgdorf with their adjutants. There was a happy moment when Adolf Hitler accepted their good wishes. Throughout 20 April a stream of visitors arrived to congratulate Hitler. Göring and Dönitz came. After a surprisingly short time Göring left Hitler's work room and the Führer-bunker. That same day he left Berlin, never to return. As soon as midnight struck, ending Hitler's last birthday, the Red Army opened its major offensive against Berlin. The Final Battle had begun.

We received the first warning signals early on the morning of 21 April. The Reich capital fell under heavy artillery bombardment. We could already hear the explosions. They rolled nearer like thundering surf. It seemed as if the excited atmosphere in the city, now fighting for its existence, immediately revived FHQ. Every man, from Hitler to the lowliest valet, knew that this was the final act. Already the Soviet shelling was hitting the government district. New craters appeared in the Reich Chancellery garden. Splinters whirred around; window panes shattered. The air was filled with dust and smoke.

At the situation conference, the senior men of the close entourage led by Keitel, Jodl and Bormann pleaded with the Führer once more to use the aircraft waiting to transfer him and his command staff to the safety of the Obersalzberg. From there it would be easier to direct the final battle than from a Berlin surrounded by the Russians.

Hitler rejected this proposal, declaring that irrespective of how the situation might develop, he would not leave the Reich capital. Since he had been in Berlin he had always made this plain to his senior officers. On his orders all aircraft at readiness were to be used to fly out women and children. Furthermore he had given all his employees permission to leave Berlin if they so desired.

Despite the heavy artillery fire and enemy anti-aircraft batteries, an overloaded aircraft managed to gain height and get clear of the Russian frontline before heading south. In-house employees and stenographers, female secretaries and members of the personal staff were amongst the passengers. Even Dr Morell, Hitler's former personal physician, made his escape from the besieged city by this means. He was too sensitive for the situation and had become very anxious. As a result of this, Hitler ordered him to go. Once Morell had left, Hitler said he would do without a physician because he did not trust them any more. He had the feeling that one of his doctors might dope him up with morphine so that he could be spirited out of Berlin against his will. Since his personal pilots, Flugkapitän Hans Baur and Flugkapitän Georg Beetz, had remained at FHQ, he also suspected that against his wishes their two reserve aircraft were being held in wait for him at Gatow airport.

The departure of Morell left the post of the Führer's personal physician vacant, and the attending surgeon, SS-doctor Ludwig Stumpfegger was appointed the successor to Morell, but he was never summoned to treat Hitler.

Although everybody – so far as I can determine – was resolved to remain loyal to his oath to the last hour, we were also strongly affected by passing events. I recall the great shock we all felt when Hewel, the foreign minister's liaison officer to the Führer, read us a leaflet by the famous Russian poet Ilya Ehrenburg. These leaflets had been dropped by Russian aircraft for distribution amongst their troops as they crossed the German border. Hewel had obtained one of the leaflets from a Russian POW (prisoner of war), and had had it translated. He read it to the members of Hitler's close circle that day in the Führer-bunker, and the words have remained imprinted indelibly in my memory. After the war I discovered that Hewel shot himself in the cellar of the Schultheiss Brewery on Berlin's Schönhauser-Allee after the break-out from the Reich Chancellery. Mentioning the Ehrenburg leaflet, Hewel had previously promised to take his own life to avoid capture. If I recount such details here, I do so in order to provide the most accurate impression possible of the mood that animated the men in the last FHQ.

*

The Russians were closing the noose around Berlin ever tighter. The battle for the Reich capital became fiercer. We learned of heavy losses amongst the civilian population. The trams, underground and surface railway systems continued to operate, though naturally not all. Where there was still electric current and an intact track, the employees, men and women, did their duty like soldiers. Even a large number of factories kept working. The men and women of Berlin went to work under Russian artillery fire. Under the deluge of shells, Berliners held firm and calm just as they did under the heavy bombing. Until the last Berlin tram stopped running, every inhabitant of the Reich capital made a superhuman effort.

The defence of Berlin continued. Goebbels did not wish to leave the capital and intended to remain with his family, so he and his wife took over Morell's former room, while their children were lodged in the old bunker. The bombardment caused serious damage to the Reich Chancellery structure. Most of the telephone connections were destroyed. On one occasion the Führer-bunker was cut off from the outside world for several hours. The communications people worked to replace the cables despite the Russian artillery fire. Manservants acted as despatch runners. In the early morning of 24 April a large part of my vehicle park was wrecked by Russian shelling. Sixty vehicles were rendered unserviceable. As the concrete roofing caved in, everything was reduced to a chaotic tangle of twisted iron and rubble.

We were surprised by the unexpected visit of Minister Speer, to see the Führer. Speer had taken his final leave of us on 20 April as he was departing from Berlin, as instructed. Now he had flown back in a Fieseler-Storch on the 25th and landed on the East–West axis. From there he had walked to the Reich Chancellery. After a long talk with Hitler he had a conversation with Foreign Minister Ribbentrop, urging him to leave Berlin. As a result, Ribbentrop took his own car and left the city successfully heading northwards. We all had the presentiment that extraordinary events were in the offing, and they began in the late afternoon, when a telegram arrived from Göring on the Obersalzberg. In great indignation we listened to its contents, which said more or less:

> Since you, mein Führer, nominated me to be your successor in case you were no longer in a position to handle the affairs of State in the event of your death or other circumstances, I consider that the time has come to take office as your successor. Should I have received no answer from you by midnight on 26 April 1945, I shall assume that you are in agreement with my action. Signed Göring.

Within the small circle to whom the contents of this telegram were known, it came as a bombshell. Since the failure of the Luftwaffe leadership, there had been a poor relationship between Hitler and the Reichsmarschall, as we knew. None of us had dreamed that Göring would send such a message, however, for he was almost dictating to Hitler. We simple men considered that what Göring was doing amounted to high treason. Things now came to a head. Shortly after the telegram arrived, the personal adjutant SS-Gruppenführer Schaub left for Munich in the last but one available aircraft. I heard that Hitler had told him to destroy all of Hitler's personal files in Munich and on the Obersalzberg. This had already been done in Berlin.

The depressed mood in the bunker began to assume a more serious aspect. Pale of face but almost astonishingly calm, the men and women there worked on. The war was considered lost. Everybody took the view that Germany was beyond salvation. Or could General Wenck still succeed in relieving Berlin?

After Schaub flew out, there was a conference between Hitler and Bormann. Declaring that he was acting on Hitler's behalf, Bormann sent the following message to Göring:

Your intention to take over leadership of the State is high treason. Traitors are punished with death. In consideration of the services you have rendered by your activities for Party and State over the years, the Führer will not impose the death penalty, but demands your immediate retirement on the grounds that by reason of ill-health you are no longer in a position to satisfactorily perform your duties. Signed Bormann.

At the same time Bormann sent a cable with approximately the following contents to SS-Obersturmbannführer Dr Frank, commanding the SS units on the Obersalzberg: 'Göring has treasonable aims. I order you to arrest Göring immediately in order to prevent all possibilities. Advise compliance here. Signed Bormann.'

Shortly afterwards, Bormann followed this up with another telegram to the Obersalzberg: 'If Berlin capitulates, the traitors of 22 April 1945 are to be shot. Signed Bormann.'

Long after the war I found out what action had been taken on receipt of these messages. Frank had immediately occupied all relevant buildings on the Obersalzberg with his three companies of Waffen-SS and hermetically sealed the entire complex from the outside world. Even the Obersalzberg RSD office was brought under his control. For security reasons, Göring was taken into Austria where he remained Bormann's prisoner until arrested by the Americans.

Chapter 8
The End Approaches

A FEW WEEKS BEFORE HITLER'S last birthday, Eva Braun had come to Berlin. Against his will, she spent his birthday with him, and the last days until his death. Not until 26 April did I find an opportunity to have a long talk with Eva Braun, whom I had known well since 1932. Calmly and with composure she confided to me her decision to remain in Berlin. At this time she was convinced that there was no way out of the situation. 'Under no circumstances will I leave the Führer, and if I have to I shall die at his side. Initially he insisted that I should take an aircraft out of Berlin. I told him: "I shall not! Your fate is also mine!"'

We were talking about Bormann who happened to be passing at that moment. Eva Braun let me know that the Führer had long seen through him, but it had been impossible during the war to winkle him out of his position of power because Hitler found it very difficult to accustom himself to new close colleagues. She said she thought the day would otherwise have come when Bormann would have been dismissed.

The Führer-bunker had already received some direct hits, but the thick concrete roofing held. The Reich Chancellery sentries were equipped with machine pistols and hand grenades to repel paratroops or assault troops. Street fighting raged in the north of Berlin. The few German troops and the Volkssturm, poorly equipped, put up a desperate defence. The enemy superiority in men and materials was too great. Our hopes for the arrival of Wenck's Army and Steiner's Panzer Corps came to nothing.

Officers and runners reported that the streets were littered with the wounded and dead. Burning vehicles and tanks indicated the severity of combat. The rooms of the New Reich Chancellery, which had previously been used as an air-raid shelter for the children of north Berlin and pregnant women, were converted into a military hospital. The constant stream of wounded enabled even those of us in Hitler's immediate circle to be kept constantly updated as to the situation in the individual defensive sectors. Often I accompanied Dr Haase, one of Hitler's former travelling physicians, on his tours of the hospital and visited my wounded SS comrades there.

Luftwaffe General Ritter von Greim, who had been appointed commander-in-chief of the Luftwaffe in place of Reichsmarschall Göring, now flew to Berlin on Hitler's order. After an intermediate stop at Gatow, the Fieseler-Storch, piloted by Hanna Reitsch, landed near the Brandenburg Gate on the East–West Axis on 26 April. Greim had been wounded by Russian fire while flying the aircraft and had collapsed in his seat; under the most difficult circumstances, his female passenger had taken over the controls and put the aircraft down successfully.

Immediately after he had reported in Berlin, the wounds of the new Luftwaffe C-in-C were dressed and painkillers administered while Reitsch informed the Führer about the flight. He was astonished at the bravery and achievements of this woman. Her skill as an aviator had always aroused his admiration. As Ritter von Greim was escorted to Hitler's ante-room, she was just taking her leave of the Führer. I had the great pleasure of speaking to her, and afterwards she spent a couple of hours with the Goebbels' children, helping them through a few difficult hours. That same woman who had achieved heroic feats and shown the highest manly bravery was now the motherly figure. She told the children fairy stories, sang and played with them and for a while made them forget their sad predicament.

At five in the afternoon of 27 April 1945, Himmler's liaison officer to Hitler, SS-Obergruppenführer and General der Waffen-SS Hermann Fegelein, phoned me to ask if I would put at his disposal two vehicles for a reconnaissance. Moreover he would be grateful if I would do him a personal favour. He wanted me to take care of a briefcase with important files belonging to the Reichsführer-SS and himself. He would hand it to me personally towards ten that evening in the Führer-bunker. It was essential to keep it safe and in the event that the enemy entered the bunker, the briefcase was to be hidden where it could never be found, or should be destroyed. Under no circumstances must it fall into enemy hands.

As I had been on familiar terms with Fegelein for years and he enjoyed Hitler's fullest confidence as Eva Braun's brother-in-law, I had no hesitation in agreeing to his request. I had really no idea at that moment that my willingness to be of assistance to him was putting my own life in danger. A short while afterwards Fegelein left the Reich Chancellery with two vehicles I had had repaired. They were the last survivors to remain serviceable from my once great vehicle fleet. To my great surprise the two automobiles were returned thirty minutes later, although without Fegelein. The drivers told me that he had got out in the Kurfürstendamm district to proceed on foot. He had left the Reich Chancellery in his Waffen-SS general's uniform.

When I reached the Führer-bunker at about thirty minutes before ten, as previously agreed with Fegelein, I found the place in uproar. An important report by the German press agency, the DNB (Deutsche Nachrichtenbüro), repeating a Reuter's bulletin, had just been made known. As no Reich Chancellery signals installations were functioning, a radio wagon from my front-convoy had been operating a makeshift service for some days from the coal bunker. Without this unit, the Führer-bunker would have been cut off from the outside world entirely for telecommunications traffic. The bunker staff worked at a feverish pace at the equipment to provide us with the text of the relayed report:

> Reuters reports through DNB that Himmler has been in contact with Count Bernadotte in order to negotiate a separate peace with the Western Allies. As the basis for negotiations, Himmler had explained that the Führer is under siege and also suffering from a brain haemorrhage. He is no longer in control of his senses and is not expected to live for more than another forty-eight hours.

It was like being struck down by lightning. This report had a much more devastating effect than Göring's telegram. Bormann came out of the situation room holding the paper in his balled fist. Outraged he said: 'I always knew that one's loyalty should not be worn on the belt buckle, but in one's heart.' (The words 'My honour is loyalty' were engraved on the SS belt buckle.) His first question to me was: 'Where is Fegelein?'

I reported my conversation with Fegelein truthfully, and of his departure with my vehicles. I added that he had wanted to hand me a briefcase at 2200 hrs. Although everybody, male and female, was making the effort to remain composed, the inner nervousness of all was obvious. The female secretaries and diplomat Hewel even asked Hitler for poison. (It was known that some time previously Himmler had given cyanide ampoules to Hitler.)

For us all, Fegelein had been an officer beyond reproach. He wore the highest decorations of the Third Reich. He was on the most familiar terms with Bormann and SS-generals Rattenhuber and Baur, as well as myself. Where was Fegelein now? If anybody knew about Himmler's treason, that man was Fegelein! Meanwhile his adjutant had returned to the Reich Chancellery where he was arrested at once by the head of the RSD Office to the Führer, Peter Högl. The adjutant made a statement to the effect that Fegelein had decided to send the two vehicles back and continue on foot. They had gone to Fegelein's Berlin flat on the Kurfürstendamm, where the general changed into civilian clothes and suggested that his adjutant do the same. The adjutant had been reluctant to do this because he thought Fegelein was acting strangely. He considered it the right thing to do under the circumstances to return to the Reich Chancellery in uniform. It was Fegelein's intention to stay put until the Russians had rolled past and then slip through their lines to join Himmler. This was obviously desertion and treason. On Bormann's order all military centres which could still be contacted were instructed that Fegelein was to be arrested on sight and brought at once to the Führer-bunker.

The following is typical for the extraordinary tempo at which events in the Reich Chancellery played out at that time. While everybody waited for Fegelein to be found, two of the manservants were married by State Secretary Naumann in the presence of Hitler and Bormann. From somewhere within the city the two girls had fled before the Russians to their fiancés for protection and help. The weddings were held in a quiet room of the Old Reich Chancellery not exposed to the artillery bombardment and where no exterior sounds reached.

Towards midnight the telephonist connected Fegelein, calling from somewhere in Berlin, to Eva Braun. In haste he urged his sister-in-law to leave Berlin with Hitler. He still considered escape possible and wanted to organise it for them. Eva Braun turned down the suggestion and rejected his help. Drawing his attention to the consequences of his actions, she insisted that he returned to his duties. Fegelein, declined, emphasising that he would not be coming back: he had made an irrevocable decision to join Himmler.

Annexed to the coal bunker were several cellars in which various people from Hitler's close circle, amongst them Fegelein, had their private rooms. The coal bunker was overflowing with civilian refugees. Shortly before midnight a suspicious-looking civilian was seen heading for the exit apparently having come from the cellar rooms to the rear. Believing this might be a saboteur attempting to escape from the coal bunker into Voss-Strasse, a refugee pointed him out to a sentry, who held the man for questioning. The suspect stated that he was General Fegelein and objected to being manhandled. The sentry knew that Fegelein was a wanted fugitive and was not intimidated. He went through with the arrest and brought Fegelein before the citadel commander, SS-Brigadeführer Mohnke. Wearing slippers and leather coat, shawl and sporting hat, Fegelein created an odd impression when we saw him in Mohnke's custody. He admitted that he had returned to fetch his briefcase from his quarters behind the coal bunker.

Mohnke handed him over at once to RSD chief Högl for interrogation. Files relating to the traitorous activities of Himmler and Fegelein, on which the Reuter report was based, were found in the briefcase. Under questioning he admitted that he intended to leave the Reich Chancellery again carrying the briefcase. During a search of Fegelein's room a trunk was found containing two half-metre-long ingots of gold of British origin and packets of pound sterling and US dollar banknotes. A superficial estimate put the equivalent value at around a million Reichsmarks. (In this connection, it is of historical interest that this trunk almost certainly fell into the hands of the Soviets when plundering the Reich Chancellery.)

Hitler ordered an immediate court martial. After a brief hearing, the case was determined on the evidence of the seized files: death by firing squad for high treason. Fegelein accepted his sentence impassively. The judgement was presented to Hitler for his confirmation and signature. He hesitated. This was a man who had proved himself at the front and was also the brother-in-law of the woman he loved. Hitler considered whether he should commute the death sentence to atonement at the front. This would give Fegelein the opportunity for rehabilitation.

Eva Braun reminded Hitler of the telephone conversation she had had with her brother-in-law a few hours earlier, and suggested that it might have been the plan of Himmler and Fegelein to deliver Hitler and herself to the Allies. She wanted to leave family relationships out of the matter: justice was justice. Without further deliberation, Hitler signed the death warrant, and SS-Obergruppenführer Fegelein was led out immediately to the garden of the Foreign Office by his own SS men for his execution.

In view of the deteriorating situation, Hitler gave Dr Haase the task of testing the poison which Himmler had supplied to him. It was visibly a difficult decision for him to use his favourite dog Blondi for the purpose. The German Shepherd had been his true friend and companion on many excursions and in hours of loneliness. After his recent experience of Himmler, Hitler wondered if the poison might be ineffective. In the event his suspicions were unfounded and immediately after being injected the dog lay dead on the carpet.

Anti-tank barricades had been erected some time earlier in the streets of Berlin. Heavy and light panzers were positioned in the avenues and open places, some of them dug in so that only the gun turret was at street level. Food was being distributed to the population. Despite the heavy bombardment, people queued at the shops. Food and clothing were the most important items to obtain, and the first cases of looting were reported. German flak artillery joined in the ground fighting. The enemy infantry and tanks were being reinforced to fight street by street and forced to pay for their success with heavy casualties. On 28 April 1945, Field Marshal Ritter von Greim and Hanna Reitsch left the Reich capital in the last aircraft.

For some days there had been talk within the intimate circle of the impending marriage of Adolf Hitler and Eva Braun. Many doubted that this would occur but we soon had the proof. The first preparations were made on 28 April. The ceremony was to be held in his study. Beforehand, Hitler dictated his will to personal secretary Frau Traudl Junge. It was the first time she had taken a shorthand note from him; usually he dictated to his secretaries at the typewriter. It was Hitler's political and well as his personal will and testament.

Those present at the marriage were the Goebbels family, Bormann, Burgdorf, Hewel, secretary Frau Gerda Christian, Reich Youth Leader Artur Axmann and Luftwaffe adjutant Colonel Nikolaus von Below. A registrar from the Propaganda Ministry, unknown to me, officiated. He performed his function to a backdrop of exploding shells and a bunker vibrating with all the direct hits. Nevertheless there was a festive mood amongst the celebrants. Hitler and Eva Braun stood before a table flanked by Goebbels and Bormann as witnesses. The official spoke in a quiet voice, adapting his words about marriage and the duties it imposed to correspond with the circumstances. The register was placed before the couple for signature. Adolf and Eva Hitler were now lawfully man and wife.

The assembly sat around in relaxed attitude as they had become accustomed to do on countless tea evenings. Although all anticipated that Hitler and his wife would soon die together, Hitler attempted to raise the mood in a courteous and friendly way. A lively conversation broke out. The close circle was reunited. The conversation turned to earlier experiences, and many reflected with nostalgia on the past.

Only slowly did news of the marriage leak out. Few people in Germany had ever heard of Eva Braun. Many wondered why Hitler had not married until so shortly before his death. The few of us who knew understood. Without a doubt we knew that this demure and loyal woman had been the person who stood closest to Hitler over his long years of loneliness.

Today one may assess the political personality of Hitler as one desires. In the final analysis, so far as I knew him, he was a loner. The only person who shared this loneliness with him was Eva Braun. She was a woman of the greatest modesty. She was always reserved and, with the exception of the last weeks of their lives, which she shared with Hitler, she never came to an FHQ or made herself known publicly. Hitler treated her as any honourable man from any sector of the population would treat a lady. He did not want the most loyal companion of his life to go down in history as his concubine. At the moment they married they knew that their deaths were imminent. For Eva Braun it was the wifely choice she made of her own free will, and from inner humility.

The morning of 29 April 1945 dawned. At first light, Goebbels and Bormann were summoned by Hitler to discuss the composition of the new Reich government. Goebbels was asked to take over as Reich Chancellor, to which he agreed. Grand Admiral Dönitz in his absence would become Reich President. The conference was concluded. Apparently all the arrangements were now in place. Hitler demanded that Goebbels should leave Berlin immediately with his family. This gave rise to a fresh drama. Goebbels considered this order to be some kind of slight and refused it. He would never leave Hitler so long as he drew breath. When Hitler insisted, Goebbels stated that his conscience would not allow him to leave Berlin since he was its commissioner for defence. The conversation became ever more emotional. The Führer was desperate. In his agitation he reproached Goebbels that now even he, one of his most loyal followers, was no longer prepared to obey his orders! With tears in his eyes, Goebbels turned and left the room. Shaken by the reproach, he went to his sitting room and dictated his will to secretary Frau Junge.

Towards six that evening I stood in Hitler's presence for the last time in my thirteen years of loyal service. As always, he was wearing his field-grey tunic with black trousers. He was composed and completely calm. Even I, who knew him so well, could not read from his attitude the decision he had already taken to end his life. In his right hand he held a map of the city. His left hand trembled slightly; this had begun on and off after a bout of influenza he had suffered at Vinniza in the Ukraine,* and in the final months was virtually permanent.

'How do you see things, Kempka?' I reported that with my men I was involved in the defence of the Reich Chancellery in the sector between the Brandenburg Gate and Potsdamer Platz. 'What do your men think?' To my reply that without exception they were maintaining a bearing beyond reproach and waiting for relief by General Wenck, he responded quickly: 'We are all waiting for Wenck!' For the last time he offered me his hand.

Once more duty called. The Russians had taken the Reichstag. Ever more assault troops had filtered into the zoo. My men needed me. This same night the wills prepared by Frau Junge for Hitler and Goebbels were signed. Werner Lorenz (representative of Reich press chief Dr Otto Dietrich), Colonel von Below and SS-Standartenführer Wilhelm Zander (Bormann's personal adjutant) were ordered to break out, each carrying a copy of the completed documents. They left the besieged city in various directions in the hope of the reaching the future Reich President, Grand Admiral Dönitz.

Shortly afterwards, Bormann and General Burgdorf ordered me to send two reliable despatch motorcyclists to General Wenck

---

* Or more likely the apoplectic fit he suffered there, as described by Colonel Nikolaus von Below (Hitler's Luftwaffe adjutant) in his memoirs, *At Hitler's Side*, London 2004. (TN)

with a special message. After a great deal of effort I succeeded in obtaining two light Sachs motorcycles on which the two despatch riders left the Reich Chancellery wearing civilian clothing. 'Wenck! It is high time! Signed Bormann. Signed Burgdorf' was the laconic content of the message with which they had been entrusted. They roared through the streets of Berlin despite the shelling, following different routes from each other, heading for Ferch near Potsdam, where Wenck and his staff were believed to be.

The first rider did not get far. With great courage he reached Grunewald, still partially in German hands, where he was stopped and held by German grenadiers. Although able to show identity papers and pay book he was arrested as a deserter. The fact that he wore civilian clothes fuelled their suspicions. He was interrogated at a battalion command post. Despite the message on Wehrmacht 'Adjutant to the Führer' notepaper signed by Bormann and Burgdorf he was detained, because nobody had ever heard of either. He was taken from command post to command post, but the names of Bormann and Burgdorf were unknown to anyone. For this reason the provenance of the message for General Wenck was doubted. Early next morning he was taken by armoured half-track to the zoo flak bunker, where a telephone call to the Reich Chancellery cleared up the misunderstanding and the despatch rider was freed to return to the Chancellery. The second rider never returned and probably failed to reach his objective.

Chapter 9

The Death of Adolf Hitler

IT WAS TOWARDS MIDDAY on 30 April 1945. Russian shelling was hitting the Reich Chancellery and the government district continuously. The struggle to hold out had become fiercer. With a thunder and a crack, whole blocks of dwellings collapsed, and the streets around the Reich Chancellery were reduced to deserts of rubble.

The Führer took his leave of his staff, shaking the hand of each and thanking them for their work and loyalty to him. Secretaries Frau Junge, Frau Christian and the dietician-cook Fräulein Manziarly were invited to lunch. Hitler sat next to his wife. As he had done in the good times, he tried to keep the conversation unforced, with everybody participating. When this last meal had ended and the three ladies had withdrawn, Hitler had them recalled by his adjutant SS-Sturmbannführer Otto Günsche. In the doorway to his ante-chamber, he and Eva Braun took their leave of the three again. Frau Hitler embraced the long-serving secretaries and shook the hand of all three in parting.

Hitler also said farewell to Bormann and his SS adjutant Otto Günsche. The latter received an express order to contact me and arrange for enough fuel to immolate the bodies of Hitler and his wife: 'I do not wish to be displayed after my death in a Russian panopticon like Lenin.'

At the time I was in one of the less damaged rooms of the underground garages, having just arrived there from outside to supervise the change of the guard. At that moment my telephone rang. I lifted the receiver and announced myself. It was Günsche. 'Erich, I am desperately in need of a drink. Haven't you got a bottle of schnapps there?' This question surprised me greatly, for the last thing we wanted nowadays was alcohol. His voice was urgent. 'Well, do you?' Whatever was up? Something was obviously afoot. Well, I would soon find out, for he promised to come straight over and so I got a bottle of cognac ready for him.

I waited and waited. What was wrong now? Günsche did not arrive. I had no idea from where he had called nor where I could reach him. More than a half hour passed, then the telephone rang again. Günsche. His voice hoarse with excitement he said, 'I must have 200 litres of petrol immediately!' At first I thought this was a bad joke and told him it was out of the question. Now he began shouting, 'Petrol – Erich – petrol!'

'OK, and why would you need a mere 200 litres of petrol?'

'I cannot tell you on the phone. But believe me, Erich, I simply must have it. Whatever it takes, it must be here right now at the exit to the Führer-bunker!'

I told him that the only source was the zoo bunker, where we had a few thousand litres buried. Under the present artillery bombardment it would be certain death for my men to go there and I was not prepared to give the order. 'Wait until at least 1700, because the firing generally dies down a bit around then,' I advised.

Günsche would not agree. 'I cannot wait another hour. See how much you can collect from the fuel tanks of your damaged vehicles, and send your men at once to the exit to the Führer-bunker. And then come yourself immediately!' With that, he hung up.

With a few exceptions, the vehicles in the garage-bunkers were not burnt-out but crushed and covered with masonry from the caved-in concrete roof. In great haste I authorised my deputy to take some men at once and siphon out what petrol could be found and bring it to the place ordered. Then I hurried by the quickest route over rubble and wrecked vehicles to Günsche, to find out what had happened. At the moment I entered the Führer-bunker, Günsche was leaving Hitler's sitting room, and we met in the lobby to the situation conference room. His features had changed visibly. As white as chalk and distraught, he stared at me.

'For God's sake, Otto, what is it?' I cried, 'you must be mad, asking me to endanger the lives of a half dozen of my men to bring you petrol under this kind of artillery bombardment!' He seemed not to have heard me, went to the two outer doors and shut them. Then he turned and said: 'The chief is dead.'

It was a dreadful shock. 'How could that happen, Otto? I spoke to him only yesterday! He was healthy and calm!' Günsche was still so overcome that he could not speak. He merely raised his right arm, imitated holding a pistol grip with his fist and pointed to his mouth.

'And where is Eva?' Günsche indicated the door to Hitler's room with his hand. 'She is with him.' With some difficulty, I extracted from him the events of the final hours. Hitler had shot himself in his study with his pistol and had then fallen head first across the table surface. Eva Hitler sat at an angle, sunk against the arm of the sofa beside him. She had taken poison, but had been holding a pistol. Her right arm was hanging over the side of the sofa, and on the ground nearby was the gun. 'Bormann, Linge and I heard the shot and rushed into the room. Dr Ludwig Stumpfegger arrived in support. Goebbels and Axmann were summoned.' Günsche was stumbling over his words as he spoke.

'Who is with him now?' I wanted to know.

'Goebbels, Bormann and Linge, also Dr Stumpfegger who certified the death of them both. Axmann has left.'

At that moment one of my own men came into the ante-chamber to report the placing of between 180 and 200 litres of petrol at the bunker exit. I sent the man back. As I did so, the door of Hitler's sitting room opened and personal manservant Linge shouted desperately for the fuel: 'The petrol . . . where is the petrol?'

I replied: 'It is in position!'

Linge returned hurriedly into the sitting room. Seconds later the door opened again, and Stumpfegger and Linge emerged carrying the body of Adolf Hitler wrapped in a dark field blanket. His face was covered as far as the bridge of his nose. Below the greying hair the forehead had the waxy pallor of death. The left arm was dangling out of the blanket as far as the elbow. Behind these two followed Bormann with the dead Eva Hitler in his arms. She was dressed in a black dress of light material, her head and blonde tresses inclined backwards. This shocked me almost more than the sight of the dead Hitler. Eva had hated Bormann. He had caused her a great deal of aggravation. His intrigues for power had long been clear to her. Now in death her greatest enemy carried her to the pyre. I could not allow this and said to Günsche: 'You help carry the chief, I will take Eva!' Then without speaking I took Eva's body from Bormann's arms. Her side was wet. Instinctively I assumed that she had also shot herself. (Later Günsche told me that when Hitler's body collapsed across the table, it overturned the vase, and the water it contained flowed over Eva.)

There were twenty steps up to the bunker exit. I had not reckoned with the weight and my strength failed. I had to stop. Halfway up Günsche hurried to assist me, and together we carried the body of Eva Hitler into the open. It was around two o'clock in the afternoon.* The Reich Chancellery was being shelled by the

---

* Here, and in the place indicated by the footnote on p.65, the author states 'two o'clock' or '1400 hrs'. This must be an error. All other authorities (Bormann's telex to Dönitz, Krebs's protocol to the Russians, statements of Günsche and Linge) put the time of death between 'after 1515 hrs' and '1550'. Kempka must mean 1600 on the basis of his earlier statement to Günsche above: 'Wait until at least 1700 because the firing generally dies down a bit around then.' Günsche would not agree. 'I cannot wait another hour.' Therefore Kempka said this occurred at 1600 hrs. (TN)

THE DEATH OF ADOLF HITLER

Russians. There were explosions very close by. Numerous fountains of soil plumed up. The air was filled with mortar dust.

In haste, Dr Stumpfegger and Linge had placed the dead Hitler on the ground about three metres half-right of the bunker exit, very close to the giant cement mixer which was to have been used to thicken the Führer-bunker roof by one metre. Just as we had carried Hitler out of his sitting room, now he lay there still wrapped in the grey blanket, legs towards the bunker stairway. The long black trousers legs were pushed up, his right foot turned inwards. I had often seen his foot in this position when he had nodded off beside me on long car drives.

Günsche and I lay Eva Hitler beside her husband. In the enormous excitement of the moment we put her at an angle to him. Russian shells were exploding around us – it seemed that their artillery had suddenly doubled its bombardment of the Reich Chancellery garden and Führer-bunker at that instant. I rushed back to the shelter of the bunker, stopping for a moment, panting, waiting for the next salvoes to arrive. Then I seized a canister of petrol, ran out again and placed it near the two bodies. Quickly I bent low to place Hitler's left arm closer to his body. His untidy hair fluttered in the wind. I took off the cap of the petrol can. Shells exploded close by, spattering us with earth and dust, metal splinters whirred and whistled above us. Again we ran to the bunker entrance for cover, our nerves stretched to breaking point. Tensely we waited for the shelling in our area to die down before pouring petrol over the corpses. Then I ran out speedily and grabbed the canister. I was trembling as I poured the contents over the two bodies, and repeatedly I told myself that I could not do it, but I was conscious of it being Hitler's last order and my sense of duty overcame my sensitivity. Alongside me, Günsche and Linge carried out the same duty for Eva Hitler. Her dress moved in the wind until finally drenched by the fuel. From the look on the faces of Günsche and

Linge I saw that they too were having a grim internal struggle to obey the chief's last order.

Flying earth from exploding shells continued to spatter us. Ignoring the deadly danger I fetched one fuel canister after another from the bunker entrance until the bodies were sufficiently soaked for the last chilling act. The working of the cement mixer had created a small depression in which we had lain the bodies. The petrol collected in it and was soaked up by the clothing on the corpses. Back to the bunker for more canisters. Then the artillery bombardment increased to such an extent that it was no longer possible to leave the bunker air lock. It must have been a minor miracle that none of the exploding shells inflicted any injury. Near us in the bunker entrance were Goebbels, Bormann and Stumpfegger. None of us dared to venture forth. Out there hell raged! How should we light the petrol?

I protested at a suggestion to ignite the bodies using a hand grenade. My glance fell on a large piece of rag near the fire brigade hoses at the bunker exit. 'Get that cloth!' I shouted. Günsche grabbed it and tore it in half. It took only a second to open the petrol tin and soak the rag with the contents. 'A match!' Dr Goebbels took a box of matches from his pocket and handed it to me. I set light to the rag and once it was afire lobbed it towards the petrol-soaked corpses. As we watched, in seconds a bright flame flared up, gurgling and hissing, accompanied by billowing black smoke. This dark pall of smoke against the background of the burning Reich capital made a grisly sight. Goebbels, Bormann, Stumpfegger, Günsche, Linge and I looked on. Slowly the fire began to nibble at the corpses. For the last time, the six of us gave the Hitler salute to the dead Führer and his wife. Then, deeply saddened by the event, we returned to the bunker.

The flames devoured the petrol, but fresh fuel could not be added to the fire until it died down. We therefore had to keep pouring more petrol over the remaining parts of the body and then

*Kempka and Adolf Hitler at the
Wolfsschanze, or Wolf's Lair, in 1942.
Located in Rastenburg, near the Russian
border, the bunker served as the Führer's
Eastern Front military headquarters.*

*Hitler and Benito Mussolini prepare to
inspect the recently deployed Italian troops on
the Ukrainian frontline, August 1941.
Kempka is behind the wheel.*

Hitler visiting a
factory in Steyr,
Austria. Standing
behind him is his valet
Heinz Linge (**left**),
and Gauleiter August
Eigruber (**right**).
Eigruber was sentenced
to death in 1946 for his
involvement at the
Mauthausen
concentration camp,
located close to Steyr.

Kempka joined the
NSDAP and the SS
in 1930, and rose
to the rank of
Obersturmbannführer,
the equivalent of
lieutenant colonel.

Hitler travelling to the Reichstag session in Berlin's Kroll Opera House before the outbreak of war in 1939. In the rear of the automobile is Linge, Joseph Goebbels and Robert Ley, leader of the German Labour Front.

Hitler during the election tours of 1932. Kempka drove thousands of kilometres during the campaign, and it was during this period that a close bond developed between the two: 'One of his kindnesses was to prepare a snack for the chauffeur to ward off tiredness at the wheel. The road map on his knees, Hitler did all the navigating himself, working out the various times to ensure he always arrived on the dot.'

Hitler at Martin Bormann's wedding in 1929, where he served serve as a witness. This was perhaps the first step of Bormann's plan to cultivate his relationship with Hitler; by 1945 he had almost complete control over Hitler's affairs. Kempka remarked: 'His influence on Hitler is probably the saddest chapter in the history of the Reich.'

Reichsleiter Martin Bormann, whom Kempka considered 'the most hated and dictatorial person' in Hitler's inner circle: 'His ruthlessness knew no bounds.' Their relationship was always tense. As he was one of the last people to see Bormann alive, after the break-out from the Führer-bunker on 1 May 1945, Kempka was called before the Nuremberg Tribunal to testify that Bormann was indeed killed in a Soviet attack.

From their first meeting in 1932, Kempka was one of the very few people who was close to Eva Braun. It was Kempka who carried her body outside the Führer-bunker for cremation following her suicide. Kempka was shocked to see the hated Bormann carry her with little care and intervened to perform this grim task himself.

Above left: *Flugkapitän Hans Baur, who was personally selected by Hitler to be his pilot in 1933, remained with Hitler in Berlin until the end. He tried to convince Hitler to escape from the bunker and had a plane standing by, but the Führer refused. Baur was wounded in the break-out from the bunker and was captured by the Soviets, who held him in captivity until 1955.*

Above right: *Kempka shortly before his death in 1975, at the age of sixty-four.*

Below: *Reichsmarshall Hermann Göring at the Nuremberg War Trials. When brought before the court, he assumed some responsibility on behalf of the deceased Hitler, and was found guilty. He avoided execution by swallowing cyanide on 15 October 1946.*

Major Otto Günsche, Hitler's adjutant. It was Günsche who ordered Kempka to find the 200 litres of petrol needed to cremate Hitler.

Otto Günsche at the Friedland Camp, Germany after his return from Soviet captivity in 1956. He was sentenced to twenty-five years in a work camp, but was released after twelve years.

In July 1945, an American soldier picks up the discarded petrol cans that were probably used in Kempka's cremation of Hitler.

A Soviet officer stands in the emergency exit of the Führer-bunker overlooking the ruins of the garden of the Reich Chancellery, where Hitler was cremated on 30 April 1945.

set fire to it again. The persistency of the Russian shelling appeared to rule out a total incineration. The act of burning the corpses lasted from about 1400 until 1930 hrs.* During the course of the afternoon, under the most difficult conditions, my men supplied several hundred more litres of petrol.

Back in the bunker, meanwhile, the entire close staff had gathered. Many went up to give the dead leader and his wife the last Hitler salute. Battle-hardened veterans such as SS-Brigadeführer Mohnke (the citadel commander), General der Polizei Johann Rattenhuber and others had tears running down their cheeks. Even though many had been prepared for this event, it still came as a dreadful blow to everybody. The calm that had reigned in all situations hitherto found its end at a stroke with the death of Adolf Hitler. People were now emotional, disheartened.

The first to pull himself together was Goebbels: 'Bormann, Burgdorf, Krebs, Mohnke – I request you to attend a situation conference immediately!'

Günsche and I went to Hitler's sitting room. We were struck by the feeling of emptiness. The traces of the suicides were still visible. The pistols of Adolf and Eva Hitler lay on the red carpet. The Führer's blood lay pooled on the table and floor coverings. Also on the table lay the overturned vase. To one side was an image of Hitler's mother as a young woman. The portrait of Frederick the Great hung above the writing table.

Pensively I left the room to resume my duties. Outside the medical room I saw Frau Magda Goebbels at a table, sunk in depression. She asked me to sit with her. I noticed how deeply she still laboured under the shock. She told me of her leave-taking from the Führer: 'I fell to my knees and begged him not to take his own life. He lifted me up benevolently and explained to me quietly that

---

* See footnote on p.62.

he had no choice. Only in that manner would the way be clear for Dönitz to save something for Germany.'

In order to distract her, I began to speak of the possibility of the Goebbels family leaving Berlin. I still had three armoured vehicles at my disposal, which I had received over the last few days. These would enable me to remove her family and herself out of the danger zone. She agreed to my proposal, and I had the impression that a great weight fell from her heart. At that moment Goebbels arrived, and his wife put my escape plan to him. Goebbels was decisive in rejecting it: 'As my authorised spokesman, General Krebs will be going to General Zhukov to negotiate the free withdrawal. Should the negotiations fail, my path is clear. I shall remain in Berlin since I have no desire to wander the world as an eternal fugitive.' Goebbels turned to me: 'My wife and children are naturally at liberty to leave Berlin.' Frau Goebbels arose: 'Obviously I shall remain with my husband. The path he chooses is also mine.'

Next I went into the medical room, where Sturmbannführer Franz Schädle, head of the SS bodyguard, lay gravely wounded, and I brought him up to date with the news. During the conversation, Günsche and RSD chief Peter Högl joined us. Günsche interrupted us to give me the order of the citadel commander SS-Brigadeführer Mohnke to report that evening, 30 April 1945, at 2100 hrs to the New Reich Chancellery coal bunker with my men to embark upon the forcible break-out. Schädle stated that he would shoot himself in the head after our departure, which he did, in order not to be taken alive by the enemy. When I went to the Führer-bunker that evening to receive my orders I met General der Polizei Rattenhuber, who told me that he was quenching the fire with some of his policemen and Hitler's manservant Linge. The charred remains of the bodies of Adolf Hitler and his wife were gathered up and interred in a shallow grave at the side of the house fronting the garages.

Chapter 10

After the Burning

AT THE SITUATION CONFERENCE involving Goebbels, Burgdorf, Bormann, Krebs and Mohnke, the basis for negotiations with General Zhukov was agreed, and General Krebs then went to the Russians to parley. As he had not returned by 2100 hrs, Mohnke postponed the break-out for twenty-four hours.

Late that evening Krebs returned to the Reich Chancellery and reported to Goebbels that Zhukov required our unconditional surrender. All he had achieved was the assurance that prisoners and the wounded would be treated in accordance with the Geneva Convention. The decision was made to break out forcibly at 2100 on 1 May 1945. We had no alternative but to go through the enemy lines or die respectably as soldiers in the attempt. More and more Russian troops were infiltrating the zoo. This meant it would be difficult for us to hold our positions until the appointed hour if they decided to launch a massed attack. With this in mind, I thought of Frau Goebbels. What would become of her and her young children? She had not wanted to leave her husband and now it was too late. I considered whether there was any way at least to save the children from this chaos.

When 1 May 1945 dawned, the mood in the Führer-bunker had never been lower. In the afternoon, State Secretary Naumann came and asked me to find another 200 litres of petrol. Dr Goebbels and his wife had decided to emulate Hitler and his wife by committing suicide. Their bodies were to be burnt after the mass break-out from the Reich Chancellery. At this time the only areas still held by German troops were Belle-Allianz-Platz, Anhalter railway station, Potsdamer bridge, the Brandenburg Gate, Friedrich-Strasse station and the Schloss district.

A girl was brought into the bunker hospital of the New Reich Chancellery seriously wounded. Her dress was torn and soaked in blood. The wounds were cleaned and dressed at once. Despite the pain she made no complaint, but just lay there pale and exhausted. In a whisper she asked for her fiancé. She knew that he was one of my drivers, but did not expect him to be here with us, believing that he was on the road on a mission. She was mistaken. I relieved the man from his guard duties and had him report. As soon as she saw him she brightened up at once and even seemed to forget her pain.

The fiancé came to me with a request. It was the girl's desire that they should marry. I went at once to State Secretary Naumann, who as a judge was competent to perform marriages; it was he who had officiated at the emergency ceremonies a few days before. This time he declined on the grounds of too much work and that he could not spare the time. His own chief, Goebbels, was making the greatest demands of him. It was therefore left to me as the fiancé's immediate superior officer to marry the couple. I had the banns written up at once and told them to attend at the dietician's kitchen at 1800 hrs for the ceremony. Supported by the witnesses, the bride and groom entered the hushed room. The occasional shell exploding in the Reich Chancellery garden made a dull thud to break the festive silence. When shells hit the bunker itself the sound was similar to breaking glass. It was difficult for me to find the right words to say, but in this unimaginably difficult situation it was strangely romantic to see these two young people gaze at each other with such devotion, just as happy couples cannot avoid doing whatever the circumstances.

Shortly after the ceremony concluded I was told that the six Goebbels children were dead. Dr Stumpfegger informed me that Goebbels had asked him to inject his children with a fast-acting poison, but he had refused. Thinking of his own children, Stumpfegger could not square such an act with his conscience. Goebbels was desperate. He wanted to prevent his children falling into Russian hands at all costs. Eventually he found a doctor amongst the refugees in the coal bunker who said he understood the Goebbels's predicament and would therefore kill their children; and he did so.

We concluded the preparations for the break-out. All unnecessary baggage had to be left behind. Even some of Eva Braun's bequests, which she had distributed shortly before her death, had to be abandoned. By 2045 hrs the funeral pyres for Dr Goebbels and his wife were ready. He arranged the whole thing himself. All those who intended to escape, whether soldiers, refugees or the wounded, were assigned to various groups. The group under my own leadership had about thirty women in it. I returned to the Führer-bunker for the last time to bid farewell to Goebbels and his wife. Although their children had been dead only a few hours they were calm and resolved. Her face pained, Frau Magda Goebbels asked me to convey her love to her son Harald from her first marriage. I was to tell him of the circumstances in which his mother had died.

It had grown dark. The individual groups left the Reich Chancellery. My group crossed the dead zone of Wilhelms-Platz, went down into the underground railway tunnels and headed for Friedrich-Strasse. Walking over rails and sleepers it took us about an hour to reach Friedrich-Strasse station. We came upon an appalling sight. Exhausted soldiers, the wounded, lacking any medical attention, and refugees lay propped against the walls, on the platforms and stairways. Most had given up all hope of escaping and were totally apathetic.

I came out of the station alone to reconnoitre the opportunities for a break-out northwards. My orders were to attempt to reach Fehrbellin with my hundred-strong group. According to our information there should have been a large German fighting unit still resisting there.

A few metres behind Weidendamm bridge was a street barricade. I heard a few shots echo my way, otherwise the district seemed deserted. The few men defending the barricade reported that various groups had succeeded in breaking out, but others had been forced back with heavy losses. A glance through the barricade convinced me of the truth of this. Dead and wounded lay like dark shadows on the street. It was a grisly sight.

Further back, around Ziegel-Strasse, the Russians had lit a giant bonfire so that they could monitor Friedrich-Strasse. The men on the barricades warned that Russians soldiers were concealed in the houses and ruins on Friedrich-Strasse. With their rapid-fire weapons they mowed down everybody approaching.

After rejoining my group I nominated the Admiralty building as the permanent rendezvous point. I gave everybody the option to detach from my group and join any other for the breakthrough if they so wished.

It was about two on the morning of 2 May 1945 when a small troop approached. I recognised Bormann by his SS-Obergruppenführer's uniform. Accompanying him, I identified Naumann, SS-Hauptsturmführer Schwägermann (Goebbels' adjutant) and Stumpfegger. They had left the Reich Chancellery after us. I asked Schwägermann immediately what had become of Goebbels and his wife. He had remained with Goebbels to the end, and gave me a short report. Goebbels had shot himself and his wife took poison, as had the Hitler couple.

The highly precarious situation prevented any longer discussion. Bormann spoke of his needs with Naumann and myself. He required a panzer for his breakthrough. I told him it was doubtful that there were any in the inner city any longer. As if by a miracle after a short while the sound of tank tracks grew ever louder, coming up from the area of the city we still held. Three Panzer IV and three armoured infantry trucks arrived to our sighs of relief and pulled up at the barricade. I spoke to the commander of the leading panzer. He reported himself as SS-Obersturmführer Hansen with the remnants of a panzer company from SS-Division *Nord*,* which was heading northwards as ordered. I explained our intentions and instructed him to proceed slowly so that our group could used the panzer for protection as far as Ziegel-Strasse.

We clung like grapes against the individual vehicles. The panzers trundled slowly forward. Ducked low we followed them like black shadows. Bormann and Naumann were on the left side of the leading panzer level with the gun turret, Stumpfegger and I immediately behind them. My hair stood on end. We all knew that this was life or death. Suddenly the Russians opened up with everything they had. A second later, a hellish tongue of flame burst out unexpectedly from the flank of the panzer. Immediately in front of me, Bormann and Stumpfegger were tossed into the air by the pressure of the explosion. In that same instant, I was knocked out. Stumpfegger crashed into my body, and I was hurled away and lost consciousness.

---

* Most likely the 11th SS-Panzergrenadier Division *Nordland*, which consisted predominantly of Scandinavian volunteers and took part in the battle for Berlin.

Chapter 11

My Escape from Berlin

WHEN I RECOVERED MY senses after an unknown period of time I was still blinded by the stab of flame from the explosion. Immediately I feared that I had lost my sight. I felt around me with my hands. My consciousness began to return. Apparently the explosion threw me into the ruins of the houses along the street. I was still unable to see, so I crawled about forty metres until I reached an impassable obstruction. I felt my way along a towering wall. I was back at the barricade from where the effort to break through had originated.

Gradually I began to see shapes again. I remained crouched at the barricade entrance. After some time I was able to make out my surroundings and saw a blurry figure. I recognized Hitler's second pilot, Flugkapitän Georg Beetz. To my horror, I saw that a shell splinter had torn open his skull from forehead to the nape of the neck. He told me it must have happened when the panzer blew up, the same explosion that had tossed Bormann, Naumann, Stumpfegger and myself into the air.

Arm in arm for mutual support we headed back at a slow pace to the Admiralty building. Just behind Weidendamm bridge, Beetz felt unable to go on. I placed him on a refugee's handcart. To my great relief I noticed Dr Häusermann, a female dental surgeon on the staff of Dr Blaschke (Hitler's personal dentist), at work tending the injured. I asked her to look after Beetz, and then fetched medical supplies from the Admiralty building. Together we bandaged the seriously wounded man. It seemed out of the question to get him away from Berlin in his condition, so Häusermann promised to take Beetz to her flat locally and care for him there. Unfortunately, as I discovered later, he succumbed to his injuries shortly afterwards.

I returned to the Admiralty building convinced by my experience that it would not be possible for a whole group of people to get away. Therefore I dissolved the group, telling each individual to obtain civilian clothing at the first opportunity and then to attempt to filter through the enemy lines. That concluded my last duty as a soldier, and now I was free to seek my own escape route. Leading about seven men I ran to Friedrich-Strasse railway station and followed the tracks in the hope of reaching Lehrter station, but this was not possible because the rail embankment was under heavy enemy fire. Anxiously I reviewed the other possibilities of a route to follow, or somewhere to hide up. There was firing in all directions. We went down the embankment to where the tram tracks curved into sheds of sidings. Cautiously entering one of these sheds I came across some female and male foreign workers. They told us animatedly that we had to get rid of our uniforms immediately or we would be murdered out of hand by the Russians. One of the girls gave me some oily overalls and sent me between the rusting radiators to change and hide my uniform. My companions also received civilian clothing. While undressing I had a closer look at a wound on my right upper arm. We were totally exhausted. Nothing was more important now than sleep, from which I hoped to regain my strength.

I had hardly stretched out when I heard loud talking below and a torrent of words in Russian. I leant over the manhole and looked down towards the doorway. A mob of Russian soldiers had discovered the foreign workers. With great jubilation they fell into each other's arms, kissing and hugging. From pure exhaustion I no longer realised the danger that had arrived so unexpectedly.

The young Yugoslav girl who had given me the overalls called up to me that I should come below. I had no option but to comply. If I had not done this, all would have been lost for us. I descended to the foreign workers and Russian soldiers in the yard. With a laugh the Yugoslav girl took my hand and led me to the Russian commissar. He gave me a brief once-over and then hugged me just as I had seen him embrace the foreign workers a few minutes before. The girl introduced me as her husband. I had the 'honour' to be embraced by the commissar again. 'Tovarich! Berlin finished – Hitler finished – Stalin great man!'

The Russians brought vodka, tinned meat, bread and butter. I called for my comrades above to come down because the commissar, drunk with victory, even wanted to embrace the 'German workers'. It was rather like a crazy dream. At last the commissar led off his soldiers, no doubt feeling that he had done his duty for the Motherland.

We returned upstairs. These few moments had drained me of more nervous energy than anything we had done since the break-out. We collapsed on the floorboards – sleep – nothing but sleep, if only for a short while. For an hour we were dead to the world. Uneasy, I awoke and staggered to my feet. We were still our own masters. I shook awake my sleeping comrades and ordered them to burn at once all identification papers, documents, orders and pay books. I emptied my pockets of any paperwork, threw my SS standard on the heap and the pennant for my vehicle. All were consumed by the flames.

Now we were anonymous. None had proof of his previous activity. An hour ago we had worn uniforms of which we had been proud for as long as we could remember; now we were vagabonds. Despite ridding ourselves of our documentation, and wearing very original attire as tram workers, we knew that as a squad we could never make it through. Difficult though it was, I had to part from these loyal comrades. It was the only possibility for any of us: to try his or her luck alone.

Just as I was leaving, by sheer bad luck I ran into the same mob of Russian soldiers returning. I was greeted with great effusiveness. They were just on their way back to the covered sidings. I had no option but to join them. As we re-entered, the Yugoslav girl who had claimed me as her husband greeted us with a smile. The commissar announced that we must now have a big victory celebration. Huge quantities of alcohol were produced. The party took place below the railway tracks.

Continually my thoughts strayed to my ruined dwelling in the Reich Chancellery garden, beside whose collapsed walls lay interred the charred remains of the man to whom I had devoted my life, together with a woman, his wife, whom I had treasured and venerated. The burial had occurred no more than forty-eight hours previously. All my thoughts were still there, where I had had to perform the most difficult duty of my life. And yet – to hang on to this laughably short life to which we are so attached I had to go along with this charade with the Russians. From all sides without pause I had to answer toasts, and countless times I had to clink my glass with the Russian soldiers.

Once when I had had some time to myself I had read a good German translation of Dante's *Inferno*, although without completely understanding it. At the time I smiled and told myself that ultimately all great writers are just fantasists. No longer so sober as he had been, the commissar insisted I should dance with my 'Yugoslav wife'. During this dance I noticed that I was bleeding from the wound in my right arm. To prevent this being noticed I put my hand in my pocket. Even these dreadful hours in the Inferno, which I have no pleasure in recalling, finally ended. That brave young Yugoslav girl, who had nothing in common with an SS officer other than sympathy born of the circumstances was the truest of true friends that day. Many men would do well to use her as a shining example of humanity. She led me, and a Hungarian baroness who joined us on the way, through all the Russian checkpoints, from where the Russians fanned out to comb the ruined city for German soldiers, to Tegel and safety. There she simply left us and returned to her people. It remains a mystery to me what this strange girl saw in me. Perhaps she had found happiness as a foreign worker in Germany.

On 30 May 1945 I reached Wittenberg. After swimming the Elbe, I went through Weimar, Nuremberg and Munich towards Berchtesgaden. Nobody knew me or interfered with me. On the way I had another enormous piece of luck. A German girl recently employed by the Allies as an interpreter managed to get me identification papers in my own name. With these I could reach my goal, Berchtesgaden, without hassle. There I spent a day and a half with my wife, recovering from the terrible strain to which I had been subjected. Nobody bothered about me – perhaps recompense for never having intentionally done anybody any harm in my life. No matter where one is nor in what century, it is always the case that after a collapse the spirit of the times will not allow malign influences to rest. It was my intention – after convalescence – to report myself to the occupation authorities as the 'head of the motor pool of the Führer and Reich Chancellor'. That was my duty, and I was fully conscious that I had to do it.

Germany's greatest writer, Goethe, who understood the world, said: 'The worst swine of all is he who denounces.' I was fingered. The following night the US Counter-Intelligence Corps came for me. After twelve hours of interrogation I was thrown into the jail at Berchtesgaden.

Now began an era in my life when I was moved from one POW camp to another. The Allies thought that Hitler was still alive. At every camp the competent officer had the sole ambition of establishing, by means of everlasting questioning, what had become of the Führer and his closest staff. This objectively very laudable ambition was a torment for me. The same questions over and over. Always the same traps rigged to ensnare me. I was not badly treated though. In general, the Americans respected my former rank of SS-Obersturmbannführer, equivalent to lieutenant colonel, and were very decent and open with me. Yet none of them could imagine how a man like Adolf Hitler could just simply die, as the facts appeared to force them to believe. They took my word for it about the death of Goebbels, for Russian propaganda had confirmed finding his body, and those of his wife and children, but the possibility that Adolf Hitler had declined to avail himself of any of the thousand opportunities open to him – no, here Erich Kempka must be lying.

'When interrogated by the CIC, a German U-boat commander said that his boat lay at Bremen at the Führer's disposal ready to sail from 25 April 1945 onwards. He stated that at least ten other U-boat commanders had been given the same order. What is your opinion on that, Herr Kempka?' I could only give a weary smile. 'We have heard from twelve pilots that they had secret orders from Führer-HQ to be at readiness to fly Adolf Hitler abroad.' In order to make their interrogations more interesting, some idiots or fantasists had actually claimed to have taken Hitler and his wife abroad.

During these dozens of interrogations I would always remember a conversation I had with Hitler in 1933, shortly after the seizure of power. I was driving him from the Reich Chancellery on the second or third occasion. At the time the words struck me as queer and I never forgot them: 'Do you know, Kempka, I shall never leave here alive!'

Perhaps all epochs have their illusions. For a person such as myself – and until I breathe my last I will never forget seeing on that April afternoon the petrol being poured over the body of the man whom I had so esteemed and honoured – they were just words that made no sense at the time I heard them.

Often the questions they asked appalled me: 'When he got up in the morning, did Hitler stand on his left leg or his right leg first? Did he hold his fork in the left or right hand?' They were rather like children asking you to explain the meaning of a fairy tale. Certainly they had been ordered to follow this line of questioning, and there was no intention to give offence. For them, Hitler had been the most fearsome and yet most interesting phenomenon of the century.

At the end of June 1946, a jeep brought me from the POW/internment camp at Darmstadt to the Nuremberg Trials. They had not known where they held me, and had had to broadcast two days of radio appeals before I was discovered. Before being taken from the prison to court, an American officer inspected my clothing. He was very correct. Apparently I was better dressed than Julius Streicher, editor of *Der Stürmer*. The only thing I lacked was a decent tie. On his order I was given a new one. I spent the afternoon in a guarded waiting room. Nobody took down my statement. After five in the afternoon I was returned to my cell without explanation. The night was difficult. A small searchlight was hung in the viewing flap in the door, and shone on my face all night.

Next morning towards eleven I was taken to the court and sworn in. They wanted to know a lot, and they were astonished that I knew so much. During the cross-examination, the US prosecutor remarked to me: 'It is a funny thing that you, of all people, happened to be everywhere.' For me, it was not funny at all. Nearly all my comrades who had experienced the death of Hitler and his wife, of the Goebbels family, of Bormann and Naumann, were either dead or in Soviet captivity. For me as somebody who had found himself in a very special position of trust *vis-à-vis* the former Führer and Reich Chancellor, it was more than a bitter pill to be exposed to such a cross-examination about my dead chief.

I had nothing to hide. I was a young man from a middle-class background with no pretensions to scholarship. I had led my life following my beliefs, honestly held. These men, the accused, had always been decent and kind to me. I would have been a swine had I allowed some crafty trick in cross-questioning to have lured me into stating something at variance with the truth. Despite everything, I was shown sympathy by one of the highest American justice officers at Nuremberg and that is something that gives me hope for the future.

In those crazy years now behind us, good and evil became intertwined. During the war I held a book in my hands in which Churchill himself had stated in the Foreword: 'Perhaps Adolf Hitler is the greatest European who ever lived.' It is not for me to deliver an opinion on the Nuremberg Trials. The Führer often told me that it is the business of the future to judge the past. We live today (1950) in the present.

I was held for weeks in the witnesses' wing at Nuremberg. There I saw once more many old comrades from better days. One for whom I had never had any time had grown into a true man; others I had respected were now Allied lapdogs. We had little opportunity to talk, but the few words we exchanged taught me more than the twelve years of conversations we had had together. Thus it was difficult then to maintain my belief in the inherent goodness in people.

As I have said in this memoir, it is not my purpose to decide between right and wrong. As a simple man, what mattered to me was how men proved their class. Almost without exception those around Hitler enjoyed only the best from him. As he used to tell me as he sat in the passenger seat beside me, often he had kept people on against his better judgement because he believed in their inner decency. I cannot condemn him for this, but perhaps history will make this its greatest reproach of him, that he was too trusting of those around him.

From Nuremberg I was brought to Langwasser camp to be discharged as a POW. Its function in this regard had ceased, and so I went to Regensburg camp for transfer from POW to internee status. On a drive from Regensburg to Ludwigsburg I was involved in a serious accident in the transport vehicle as a result of which, following court proceedings, I was released in October 1947.

I know that many Germans had to go through terrible times. I also know that Adolf Hitler today is one of the most controversial personalities in history. Only later generations will be able to form a precise assessment of this man.

Appendices

The Historical and Social Context of the Period
by Erich Kern

Appendix 1

In the Bunker for the Last Battle

ALTHOUGH AWARE THAT HIS defeat was probably approaching, Hitler decided to continue resisting to the last and to die in the Führer-bunker; secretly he cherished the hope that, as with Frederick the Great, the fates would turn in his favour at the last moment. Merely thinking of this man, the army commander of the Prussians, stiffened Hitler's resolve. Repeatedly he would refer to Frederick as the model soldier. Just as Frederick had not earned his suffix 'the Great' from his victories, but because he was not dismayed by misfortune, so would posterity see his, Hitler's, significance because he also never gave in despite the severest reverses. This he explained to Ferenc Szálasi on 4 December 1944.[*]

After summoning the Gauleiter and Reichsleiter before him for the last time on 24 February 1945, Hitler concluded his talk by mentioning his failing health and compared his own situation to that of Frederick the Great, who returned from his own wars an infirm and broken man: 'My leg trembled,' he told them, 'and now it's my arm, perhaps one day my head will wobble. But of one thing I can assure you: my heart will never wobble.'[†]

---

[*] David Irving, *Hitler und Seine Feldherren*, Frankfurt 1975, p.669. Published in English as *Hitler's War*, London 1977.

[†] Gauleiter Rainer, quoted in A. Hillgruber, H. Greiner & P.E. Schramm (eds), *Kriegstagebuch des Oberkommandos der Wehrmacht* (hereafter 'KTB OKW'), vol. IV, Frankfurt 1969.

The two men who were there, the former Gauleiter Rudolf Jordan and Karl Wahl, described this tragic scene in their memoirs. Jordan stated:

> Once again Hitler appealed for all moral and material reserves for the decisive hours. He ended with the admission that Fate had not called us to be the last of a great German past, but pioneers of a greater future now beginning, for us who were now hardened by the greatest of all wars of history. We rose quietly to give the salute – and recognised that this was no longer our Hitler as we had known him but a man battered and almost broken by the political, military and not least human tides – a beaten man, lonely, abandoned, already perched on the ruins of his work without yet having become fully aware of it.[*]

Karl Wahl wrote:

> For the first time since I had known Hitler he spoke for a while to the assembly about his ill-health, apparently feeling that he should do so because he could no longer hide it. At this time, Hitler was less an ill man than a depleted, drained individual, though just as body and soul are almost inseparable, Hitler's mind was still fully intact. As I learned later from eyewitnesses in Hitler's circle, it remained the case to his death despite his precarious health.[†]

The Hitler of that time can be compared to a fatally wounded tiger, which despite its injuries still has great strength in its claws. David Irving said of him: 'His sharp mind kept working both logically and flexibly.'[‡]

---

[*] Rudolf Jordan, *Erlebt und Erlitten*, Leoni, Bavaria 1971, p.256.

[†] Karl Wahl, *Patrioten oder Verbrecher*, Offenbach 1975, pp.160f.

[‡] Irving, *Hitler und Seine Feldherren*, p.706.

Hitler's secretary Traudl Junge noted how he embraced the example of Frederick the Great to the last. Hitler said that the outcome of a battle depended on the last battalion and quoted as examples Waterloo and Kunersdorf. If he succeeded in thwarting the Russians at Berlin, that would give the Germans new heart just as the Battle of Stalingrad had given the Russians new heart. Moreover, Hitler hoped that a rift might open between the Soviets and the Anglo-Americans, making a conflict between them unavoidable. That would be the moment in which he, Hitler, would strike.[*]

On 12 March 1945 Hitler issued the notorious order for the destruction of property, the main purpose of which has been ignored or minimised by historical research. It was aimed at property: 'that might be useful to the enemy for the continuation of the campaign immediately or in the near future'. If the order were to have been obeyed everywhere, then naturally the German people would have suffered major damage to property, but from a military point of view it was logical.

Hitler was expecting Stalin's major offensive on the Oder front. The Red Army was superior to the exhausted German one in materials, but General Schörner had more than 410,000 men and Colonel General Heinrici more than 527,000. General Theodor Busse was almost certain that his Ninth Army could ward off the Soviet push on Berlin. On 4 April, with Heinrici, Hitler looked over many kilometres of the defensive front on the Oder and ordered the laying of minefields, and for the Ninth Army, which had the task of holding the strategic Seelow Heights, the excavation of subterranean galleries as a shelter for troops against Soviet artillery barrages.

But now, in the shadow of apparently unstoppable defeat, the will to fight on began to die, even amongst the majority of the generals who had never been part of the [Stauffenberg] conspiracy. Hitler's orders were now carried out mostly half-heartedly, or

[*] Nerin E. Gun, *Eva Braun-Hitler*, Kettwig 1968, p.194.

only ostensibly. Nobody was keen to die a hero's death only weeks before the end. Thus in the final phase of the drama, Hitler and his generals began to drift apart slowly but surely. David Irving wrote:

> But which generals still followed Hitler's orders? His authority was weakening, and they began to act based on their own assessment of the situation, either understanding incorrectly, or in total ignorance of, the central strategy being decided in Berlin. 'Blomberg told me that obedience stopped short at the generals,' Hitler recalled a few days before the end.[*]

The German officers and men at the front, who had to look on as the Red Army soldiers indulged in murdering, raping, plundering and robbing the German civilian population, had ceased to speculate about tomorrow. They stood and fought in the most exemplary manner. Exceptional conduct became the rule. The Red Army in February 1945 alone lost 4,600 tanks, twice the Soviet monthly production. In the first three weeks of March, 5,452 Russian tanks were destroyed.

On 12 April 1945 US President Roosevelt died of apoplexy at Warm Springs. This report gave rise to great hopes in the Führerbunker, especially for Goebbels. It was now generally felt that the war had entered a decisive phase. The Western Powers had to brake the Communist advance through Europe if they were to prevent the loss of all Europe to the Russians. Even Hitler succumbed to this illusion, remarking: 'You see, therefore the war is not lost.'[†]

With the last of his physical strength, Hitler turned all his attention to confronting the Red Army. That for the most part his orders were no longer being followed is another matter entirely.

---

[*] Irving, *Hitler und Seine Feldherren*, p.707.
[†] Irving, *Hitler und Seine Feldherren*, p.711.

On 15 April 1945 Hitler made his last address to troops on the Eastern Front:

> For the last time, the Jewish–Bolshevist arch-enemy is sending its hordes into the attack. Their intention is to reduce Germany to rubble and exterminate our people. You soldiers from the East particularly understand the fate that threatens above all our German women, girls and children. While old men and children are murdered, women and girls are debased in military brothels. The remainder are transported to Siberia.
>
> We have prepared for this hour, and since January everything has been done to erect a strong front. The enemy will encounter very powerful artillery. Losses amongst our infantry have been made up by numerous new formations. Rapid response units, new divisions and the Volkssturm are reinforcing our front. The Bolshevist will experience the old disasters of Asia, that is, he must and will bleed to death before the capital of the German Reich.
>
> Whoever fails to do his duty at this time is a traitor to our people. The regiment or division that deserts its position will stand disgraced before the women and children who face daily the terror bombing of our cities. Beware above all the few traitorous officers and men who, in order to save their own miserable lives, are in the pay of the Russians, perhaps still in German uniform, and fight against us. Whoever orders you to pull back, and is a person unknown to you, is to be detained and if necessary removed forthwith without regard to his rank.
>
> If in these coming days and weeks every soldier on the Eastern Front does his duty, the final attack will be smashed just as at the end the penetration of the West by our enemies will collapse in spite of everything. Berlin will remain German. Vienna will be German again, and Europe will never be Russian. Build a loyal community, not based on the hollow concept of Fatherland, but one to defend your homeland, your women, your children and

with it our future. In this hour, the whole German people look to you, my Eastern troops, and cling to the hope that by your dogged steadfastness, your fanaticism, your weapons and your leadership, the enemy attack will end in a bloodbath for the Bolsheviks. That moment in which Fate removes the greatest war criminal of all times from the Earth will turn the tide of this war.[*]

At the same time Hitler ordered General Busse to pull back the Ninth Army to a reserve front line, anticipating the expected Russian Great Offensive. The Ninth Army consisted of V SS-Mountain Corps (SS-Obergruppenführer Jeckeln), the fortifications at Frankfurt/Oder under Colonel Biehler, XI SS-Panzer Corps (SS-Obergruppenführer Kleinheisterkamp), an Army Corps (Lieutenant General Wilhelm Berlin) and as army reserves Panzer Division *Kurmark* and the 25th Panzergrenadier Division. As a result of the measure to pull back, the ensuing Russian artillery barrage bombarded nothing.

Then began the murderous fighting. The Red Army threw 2,000 bomber aircraft against the German infantry, which had not succeeding in repulsing the Russian armour. With fanatical commitment, the remnants of the German Luftwaffe took up the unequal struggle. Sixty kamikaze pilots dropped their bombs on to the Oder bridges in the hope of destroying the crossings. Nevertheless the Soviets drove forward eight kilometres west of the Oder, albeit with appalling losses. The brave panzer, flak and Panzerfaust grenadiers of General Busse destroyed 211 Soviet tanks, and another 106 on 17 April. On the Neisse front, the Fourth Panzer Army (General Fritz Gräser) destroyed ninety-three Soviet tanks on 16 April and another 140 the following day. On 18 April, however, Zhukov finally overcame the resistance of SS-Panzergrenadier

---

[*] Deutsche Nachrichtenbüro text, 16 April 1945.

Division *Nederland* and seized the Seelow Heights. Now the initiative lay with the enemy.

In the Reich Chancellery garden on 20 April 1945, his fifty-sixth birthday, Hitler decorated a group of Hitler Youth with the Iron Cross for their bravery with flak and ground units. A little later, he experienced one of his severest disappointments when Göring asked: 'Mein Führer, will you object if I go to Berchtesgaden now?' Hitler, initially speechless, replied: 'As far as I am concerned, just go.'[*]

Soviet units now began to fill the gaps appearing in the frontline held by Gräser's Fourth Panzer Army and Busse's Ninth Army. Only Schörner had gone over to the counterattack. Hitler ordered Heinrici to attack at once, but this order was not acted on.

As David Irving remarked:

The Army Group commander had resolved to turn away from Hitler's 'unfeasible order' and fight his way through to the west while he still had the chance. This widened the gap and eventually sealed the fate of Berlin – and also that of Hitler if he intended to remain and defend the city to the last. Hitler was under the impression that his orders were being followed.[†]

When General Hans Krebs (head of the OKH command group) and Major General Erich Dethleffsen (deputy chief of the general staff) reported that the gap had widened, Hitler replied calmly: 'Treason!' Dethleffsen, perplexed, asked: 'Mein Führer, you mention so often betrayal by the military commanders and men. Do you believe that there is really so much betrayal?' Hitler looked at him: 'All the

---

[*] Irving, *Hitler und Seine Feldherren*, p.715 per Karl Jesko Puttkamer interviews in 1967.

[†] Irving, *Hitler und Seine Feldherren*, p.716.

failures in the East are due purely to betrayal,' he responded, from deep inner conviction.*

Hitler now placed all hope in SS-Gruppenführer Felix Steiner, adding some Luftwaffe units to his moderately equipped panzer group. Steiner reported:

> Two days later (on 20 April) the corps – now redesignated an army group – received a new order. It was to relieve Berlin. Using the decimetre radio I spoke to the chief of the general staff, Krebs, from whom I learned that Berlin was to be relieved by an operation involving the Ninth Army, Twelfth Army and Army Group Steiner. I could only reply that the Ninth Army (Busse) was encircled and appeared non-operational, Wenck had no more than a couple of divisions, and I did not have even the strength of a weak corps. Then the connection was broken.
>
> I notified OKW (Army High Command) at Fürstenberg and Army Group Weichsel that I was declining to carry out the attack towards Berlin. In our condition the operation ordered appeared madness. Meanwhile large numbers of highly decorated airmen of all ranks were arriving at Liebenwalde armed only with machine pistols or assault weapons, and with these it was proposed they should engage the Soviet armour. Hitler Youth with rifles followed them. All were sent back to barracks at Mecklenburg or Holstein; it would have been irresponsible to have tossed them into the fray. Army Group and OKW insisted that I carry out the attack. Apparently they could not understand the reasons for my declining. On 22 April at 0500 hrs Field Marshal Keitel attempted to persuade me, but he did not really believe in it and was probably just going through the motions.

---

* Dethleffsen, quoted in KTB OKW, pp.1703f.

The last chief of the Luftwaffe general staff, General Koller, wrote in his dairy:

21 April 2000 hrs. Telephone conversation with General Krebs, chief of army general staff. Enemy advancing from Lübben to Baruth. Fighting northeast of Bautzen and south of Spremberg. Then I reported about Luftwaffe engagements. In the evening between 2030 and 2100 Hitler phoned. 'The Reichsmarschall is forming a private army at Karinhall. Disband it at once and occupy the place!' While I was still considering the implications, he rang again: 'Every available man between Berlin and the eastern coast stretch Hamburg to Stettin is to be co-opted for the attack ordered by me.' To my objection that we had no experienced infantry, and to my enquiry whom we were to attack I received no reply. He had already hung up. I had no expectations of an attack. In a series of telephone calls I attempted to obtain clarification. In the conversations with the Führer-bunker when trying to speak to General Krebs, Hitler suddenly came on the line. I reiterated that all the troops were raw. They were poorly equipped for ground engagements and lacked heavy weapons. Hitler then delivered a talk on the situation and ended: 'You will see, the Russians will suffer the greatest defeat in their history at the gates of Berlin.' He ignored my remark that the situation in Berlin appeared hopeless.[*]

Steiner did not move from where he was.[†]

Towards midday on 22 April, SS-Obersturmbannführer Fritz Beutler coming from Vienna brought Hitler a belated birthday present from Sepp Dietrich of the Sixth Panzer Army – a cheque

---

[*] Felix Steiner, *Die Freiwilligen der Waffen-SS*, Oldendorf 1973, pp.326f.

[†] Irving, *Hitler und Seine Feldherren*, p.721.

for more than 7.5 million Reichsmarks collected by men of his army for the Winter Relief Fund. Beutler observed:

> When I was sitting opposite Hitler on the afternoon of 22 April, he looked a wreck. Certainly the left hand and arm were trembling, but I had not expected to find him so physically decrepit, despite the frequent accounts I had received from others who saw him. What he said was clear and precise, and his observations on the military situation were accurate, at least for the area of my knowledge. He knew exactly the position of each unit.'[*]

At that afternoon's situation conference Hitler suffered a nervous breakdown for the first time. Then he dictated to Goebbels the text of an announcement that he would remain in Berlin. He brushed aside all attempts to get him to reconsider from Goebbels, Bormann, Keitel and Jodl, and Dönitz and Himmler by telephone. He regretted having left east Prussia because then the Red Army would never have achieved its breakthrough. 'I see the struggle as lost and feel cheated and deceived by those in whom I invested my trust. I am resolved to remain in the capital for the struggle against Bolshevism and to assume the defence of this city myself.'[†]

While the Red Army edged forward despite stubborn resistance offered by German ground forces, which included numerous European Waffen-SS volunteers, Jodl ordered General Wenck to about-turn his Twelfth Army to face east and so join the final battle for Berlin.[‡] At the time, the Twelfth Army comprised:

- Panzer Division *Clausewitz* (General Unrein)
- Infantry Division *Potsdam* (Major General Berg)

---

[*] Uwe Bahnsen & James O'Donnell, *Die Katakombe*, Stuttgart 1975, p.146.

[†] Irving, *Hitler und Seine Feldherren*, p.719.

[‡] Heinz Guderian, *Erinnerungen eines Soldaten*, Heidelberg 1951, pp.388f.

- Panzergrenadier Division *Schlageter*, Infantry Division Scharnhorst (Major General Götz)
- Infantry Division *Ulrich von Hutten* (Lieutenant General Engel)
- Infantry Division *Friedrich Ludwig Jahn* (Colonel Weller, later Colonel Zöller)
- Infantry Division *Theodor Körner* (Lieutenant General Frankewitz)
- Division *Ferdinand Schill* (Lieutenant Colonel Müller).

Hitler appointed General der Panzertruppe Wenck commander of the newly reconstituted Twelfth Army on 7 April 1945. It was Germany's last remaining powerful army. It carried the hopes of all in the Führer-bunker. Wenck was to reach the autobahn at Ferch near Potsdam. Meanwhile XXXXI Panzer Corps under Lieutenant General Rudolf Holste had to cross the Elbe and attack between Spandau and Oranienburg. Steiner was ordered to transfer his motorised troops to Holste.*

Hitler now wanted Eva Braun, Frau Goebbels with her children, Goebbels himself and all female secretaries to leave Berlin. All refused. They showed more backbone in these dramatic hours than many men. As if the approaching catastrophe were not enough, on 23 April Hitler received a fresh blow when Göring sent him the following signal from Berchtesgaden:

Mein Führer! Are you in agreement, following your decision to remain in the fortress of Berlin, that according to your edict of 29 June 1941 I, being your deputy, should assume immediately the overall leadership of the Reich with full freedom to act at home and abroad? If I do not receive a reply by 2200 hrs I shall accept that you have been deprived of your freedom to act, shall consider

---

* Franz Kurowski, *Armee Wenck*, Kurt Vowinckel Verlag 1967, p.161.

the provisions of the edict to have come into force and act in the interests of people and Fatherland. You know what I feel for you in these most difficult hours of my life and what I cannot express in words. God protect you and have you come here at the earliest despite everything. Your loyal, Hermann Göring.

Göring also telexed Ribbentrop with a request to come to the Obersalzberg.*

There were rumours that Göring wanted to fly to see the American commander-in-chief to request his conditions for a ceasefire. It was grotesque, for even Göring was under the same illusion created by the refined black propaganda of Sefton Delmer – first get rid of Hitler! – and despite the ceasefire terms already having been announced officially in the wake of the Casablanca and Yalta conferences. The only offer on the table was unconditional surrender and the division of Germany into three occupation zones.

Hitler replied to Göring: 'The Führer-edict of 29 June 1941 is herewith declared null and void. Your conduct and measures are a betrayal of my person and the National Socialist cause. I am fully possessed of my freedom to act and forbid all further measures. Adolf Hitler.' At the same time he made various statements relating to Göring's earlier services but insisted that he should retire from all his offices. Göring gave in and obeyed. Bormann now ordered the Obersalzberg SS unit to arrest and detain him pending trial. Hitler nominated Colonel General Robert Ritter von Greim to be the new commander-in-chief of the almost non-existent Luftwaffe.

Speer, who loathed Göring, sent a signal repeating the text of the Göring telex to Colonel Adolf Galland, whose Me 262 squadron was in Bavaria: 'This telex is clear. The Führer has responded in the appropriate manner and ordered the arrest of Göring. I request

* Telex from Göring to Ribbentrop, 23 April 1945, 1759 hrs.

that you and your colleagues do everything to prevent a flight by Göring in the sense discussed."[*]

On 23 April 1945, Hitler had leaflets prepared for men of the Twelfth Army containing the following sentiment:

Soldiers of Wenck's Army! An order of the greatest importance has called you from your areas of advance towards our Western enemy and set you heading eastwards. Your task is clear: Berlin must remain German! The objectives required of you must be achieved at all costs, for operations are afoot from other directions intended to strike a decisive blow against the Bolsheviks in the battle for the Reich capital, and bring decisive change to the situation in which Germany presently finds herself. Berlin will never capitulate to Bolshevism. The defenders of the Reich capital have taken fresh heart upon hearing news of your rapid approach, and are fighting on doggedly and with great determination in the hope of soon hearing the thunder of your guns. The Führer is calling you. You are on the attack as in the old victorious days. Berlin awaits you. Berlin is anxious to greet you warmly.

General Wenck did not distribute the leaflets, but had them incinerated.[†] On 24 April, Hitler appointed General Helmut Weidling battle-commandant of Berlin. Contact with him had been lost for a lengthy period previously to the extent that it was suspected he might have defected to the Soviets. By now affairs had come to a pretty pass and the allotted task was beyond him. Weidling did what he could, but he was particularly short of artillery and panzers, and a junior officer had taken it upon himself to blow up prematurely Berlin's last great ammunition dump at Krampnitz. Weidling had at his disposal the remnants of the mauled LVI Panzer Corps and

---

* Irving, *Hitler und Seine Feldherren*, p.722.
† Kurowski, *Armee Wenck*, p.112.

fighting groups of the Waffen-SS, old Volkssturm men, police, a few thousand flak soldiers and the 2,700 boys of the Hitler Youth 'Tank-Destruction Brigade'. Dönitz promised to fly in 2,000 sailors and coastal defenders for the final battle plus another 3,500 men.

A tight defensive ring known as the 'citadel' was established around the Führer-bunker under the command of SS-Brigadeführer Wilhelm Mohnke. The boundaries of the citadel began in the north on Weidendamm Bridge over the Spree, went along the river to the east to include the museum, island, the royal palace to the Spittalmarkt, Potsdam station to Potsdam Bridge in the west, Anhalter station, through the zoo, over Grosser Stern including the Kroll Opera House and from there the circle rejoined in the north at the Spree. Mohnke's core units were Waffen-SS from the Reserve-Regiment at Berlin Lichterfelde plus men from the various Berlin central offices of the Waffen-SS. During the course of the fighting these troops were supplemented by French volunteers from SS-Division *Charlemagne*, Hitler Youth battle groups, Volkssturm and men of the three Wehrmacht services loose from their units, and police. The strength of this force was variable and never exceeded one thousand.

SS-Brigadeführer Mohnke's immediate superior was Hitler. Mohnke consulted General Weidling to coordinate the overall situation and regarding all measures. On three occasions between 23 and 30 April 1945, Mohnke had private talks with Hitler in addition to the official situation conferences. When asked about Hitler's mental state in the last days of his life, Mohnke declared: 'At all times I had the impression that Hitler was fully familiar with the subject matter under discussion and held a sober opinion on all affairs. In my personal opinion he was fully present mentally.'[*]

On 25 April, the Russians closed their circle around Berlin. Men of the Soviet and US armies embraced like brothers at the

---

[*] Written statement from Mohnke to the author, 4 August 1975.

Elbe. Eisenhower halted his advance to allow Zhukov and Koniev precedence into Berlin. This destroyed once and for all the illusion of an East–West confrontation. The only glimmer of light was the arrival of Wenck's regiments in Berlin. This had the Soviets running for their lives. The Germans in the liberated region could hardly believe it and wept for joy.

Weidling reported on the situation that day:

On 25 April I completed my assessment of the individual sectors and reviewed the confused arrangement that existed for the transmission and execution of orders, also the military centres and the Party organisation. I visited the commandant of Berlin's air defences, Lieutenant General* Sydow, who was subordinate to the Regional Defence Staff, and Luftwaffe Major General Müller, commander of all aircraft for the defence of Berlin. At Sydow's command post in the zoo flak bunker, I experienced a heavy air raid by Russian aircraft against the flak tower with its battery of twelve guns. The tall tower shook as bombs exploded close by. This was quite an unusual feeling! After seeing over the Bendler Block, I decided to install my own command post there because it was a shorter distance to the Reich Chancellery and the flak bunker was bursting at the seams with people sheltering.

There had been heavy fighting since morning at Spandau, where a unit under SS-Gruppenführer Heissmeyer, mostly Hitler Youth, was encircled; in the western harbour area, with serious casualties; and in east Berlin around Friedrichshain with variable success. The enemy was attacking with fresh troops at Zehlendorf. On the afternoon of 25 April, orders were worked out for the reorganisation of the defence of Berlin. The sectors were divided up as follows:

---

* Correctly Major General. (Author)

- **Defence sectors A and B** East Berlin (General Mummert, commanding officer, Panzer Division *Müncheberg*);
- **Defence sector C** Southeast Berlin (SS-Brigadeführer Ziegler, commanding officer, SS-Panzergrenadier Division *Nordland*);
- **Defence sector D** Either side of Tempelhof airport (C Artillery, LVI Panzer Corps, Colonel Wöhlermann replacing the former commander, sixty-two-year old Luftwaffe Major General Schreder, considered not up to the task);
- **Defence sector E** Southwest Berlin and Grunewald (since 24 April held by 20th Panzergrenadier Division);
- **Defence sector F** Spandau and Charlottenberg (remaining under Lieutenant Colonel Eder);
- **Defence sectors G and H** Northern Berlin (Colonel Herrmann, 9th Fallschirm-Jäger Division);
- **Defence sector Z** Centre (Lieutenant Colonel Seiffert).

At 2200 hrs I went to the Reich Chancellery with the situation report. The Führer was sitting behind his table with his maps (. . .) All present listened with rapt attention to my report. I began with the enemy dispositions as we had identified them over the last few days. For this purpose I had prepared a large sheet of paper sketching the enemy's directions of attack. Against each I put the number of enemy divisions, and the numbers, condition and armament of the enemy divisions at readiness in the overall defence region.

From the situation map it was obvious that Berlin would soon be encircled (which occurred on the morning of 25 April). Using a city plan, I explained the disposition of our own troops. Despite successfully warding off enemy attacks along all sectors, our frontline was being forced back slowly but surely towards the city centre (. . .)

Once I had concluded, the Führer spoke. In long, repetitious sentences he set out the reasons compelling his remaining in

Berlin. He would either triumph or go down here. Everything he said expressed the idea one way or another that if Berlin fell, nothing could stop the final defeat of Germany.

I, a simple soldier unknown amongst this gathering, stood here at the place from where in past times the fate of the German people had been determined and directed (...) I wanted to cry out: 'Mein Führer, but this is all madness! A great city like Berlin cannot be defended with the forces at our disposal and the meagre quantities of ammunition we have. Consider, mein Führer, the endless suffering which the population of Berlin will have to endure during this battle!' I was so incensed that it required an effort on my part not to blurt this out.

Another way had to be found. Initially it seemed essential to convince General Krebs of the hopelessness of pursuing it, and that could only be done gradually. Krebs delivered a summary of the general situation. That evening he presented it in a relatively optimistic manner. Three points he made impressed me very much:

1. The Ninth Army (encircled southeast of Berlin) was not attacking, in accordance with the Führer's order, to the northwest, but to the west in the direction of Luckenwalde. From this alone, anyone knowledgeable would recognise that the Ninth Army command either could not take part in the defence of Berlin, or did not intend to do so. Personally I thought that the Ninth Army with its exhausted divisions was principally interested in linking up again with Wenck's Army.

2. The broad and deep penetration by the Russians in the area of Army Group *Weichsel*. The spearheads of the Russian attack were very close to Prenzlau, and therefore this Russian attack must very soon affect the outcome of the struggle for Berlin!

3. Wenck's Army, about three and a half divisions, had carried through the anxiously awaited attack to breach the blockade of

Berlin. This was now Wenck's Army, the Reich reserve, of which Dr Goebbels had very recently spoken in a radio broadcast.

Wenck's Army now became the symbol for the liberation of Berlin. Its coming was announced not only by radio, in leaflets and the last newspaper of the Reich capital, *Panzerbär*, but also in whispered propaganda. An officer in Berlin reported that 'Hold out until Wenck's Army arrives!' was the order, and the aim was to destroy Zhukov's assault forces in the battle for the Reich capital. Under this slogan, we accepted battle for Fortress Berlin. It was positive enough to get us to throw in everything available.

Despite their success in the outer suburbs we had rendered to the Soviets nothing without a fight, and we were determined to make them pay as dearly as possible. This must have weakened them.

The house-to-house fighting in the stone labyrinths made up for what we lacked: here a courageous man armed with a Panzerfaust really was the equal of a T-34. The Soviet tanks came up with surprises – steel netting or suspension and steel plates fronting the armour to absorb some of the effect of the Panzerfaust, but we could get behind them and sheer numbers did not matter.

After the initial very one-sided frolics of the Red airforce over the city, which caused nasty losses to our precious heavy weapons, suddenly like the rays of the morning sun our own fighters appeared, and in a surfeit of numbers we had never dreamed of. It seemed to us like manna in the desert. They gave us a breathing space, literally. Our only worry now was what moved on the ground and our gunners 'had a roof over their heads'. There was suddenly a sober confidence that this battle could be won: an indescribable heartfelt tenacity, confidence in victory and a readiness to die attempting it; these had come to dominate our struggle.

Like some underground current, Hitler's belief revitalised the warriors in the bastion. We would hold out, we could hold out, longer and more certainly than we were ordered from one day to the next if only they tackled the Soviets beyond the Ring as we did inside it. A vortex of rage, a great feeling of superiority and an unlimited capability beyond words seized the defenders of Fortress Berlin. Units that yesterday had fallen back demoralised and devoid of hope were suddenly gripped by it, shaken back to life, their backbones replaced. Today they looked upon the enemy with the sniper's calm. If the Twelfth Army (Wenck) made it here, if Army Group Steiner and Schörner (whose Army Group centre had been attacking Koniev's 1.Ukraine Front on its flank since 23 April) made it, then God knew, no Bolshevist would leave Berlin alive and the ruins that we defended would become the tomb for the Red Army. Berlin will remain German! . . .

Reports on the situation: in the north near Oranienburg-Bernau, heavy fighting. To the south Schörner attacking, compressing the corridor containing the Ukraine Front for their breakthrough. In the west, the Twelfth Army has turned and is hurrying here. Should Zhukov wish to hold the city, it will cost him dear, even should we be reduced to fighting with pistols.'*

The Red Army began to encounter more determined resistance around Berlin. Every house and every ruin had its price in blood. Soviet Marshal Vasily Chuikov depicted the unbelievable ferocity of the fighting from the Russian point of view:

By the evening of 25 April, combat units of my army with their commands and sections had advanced three to four kilometres towards the city centre. The Germans fought tenaciously and with desperation whenever we met them. Every dwelling, every block of houses in the defence region had its machine-gun nests and Panzerfaust grenadiers. Many railway lines met in Berlin. They

* Peter Gosztony, *Der Kampf um Berlin 1945*, Düsseldorf 1970, pp.259ff, based on Weidling's notes in Soviet captivity, which he did not survive; German translation in *Wehrwissenschaftliche Rundschau*, No. 1/1962.

cut through the city in various directions and were exceptionally suitable for the installation of defensive positions. Approaches to stations, bridges and crossings had been reinforced into strong points; the canals and locks converted into obstacles intended to bring our attack to a stop. From every nook and cranny – in streets and alleys, from cellars and ruins – our soldiers met a deadly hail of fire.

The Germans made repeated counterattacks using panzers and SP guns. They employed the following tactic: after the counterattack, they made a feint, as though it had failed, and pulled back. In the roomy villas, troops were concealed with machine pistols. Their job was to attack our assault formations on the flanks and from the rear, causing us heavy casualties with concentrated fire. Our elite units quickly identified the ploy, intensified scouting activities and fired on the windows, roofs and doorways of even apparently abandoned houses, or tossed hand grenades inside. This forced the German MP-soldiers out of their lairs.

On the way to Tempelhof airport, our units managed to cross the Teltow Canal after heavy fighting. Soon came the report: 'The airfield is surrounded!' It was the last airport in Berlin from which it was still possible to take off. It was obvious that the Germans would do whatever they could to keep open this 'doorway' into the air. The airfield was defended by flak-, panzer- and SS units at its boundaries in a horseshoe-shape to the south and east. Most of the panzers were dug in, ready to fire. From this, we inferred that the defenders of Berlin had run out of fuel for their panzers. From panzer crews taken prisoner, we discovered that all fuel had been requisitioned by the Luftwaffe.

There was something else prisoners told us, which we had to take into account. There were underground hangars at the airport where aircraft were kept at flight readiness day and night with crews on standby. Amongst these crews were experienced pilots who had been entrusted earlier with flying Hitler, Goebbels,

Bormann and other major personalities of the Third Reich. From this information one assumed that Hitler and his closest colleagues were still in Berlin. Should the devil so wish, they could make use of this 'doorway' out of the rubble at any moment. Something had to be done to prevent that happening. If we were too hasty we might make them dig in deeper, yet a delay in the attack would have been an unforgivable error, for then the principal war criminals might have made their escape. Therefore we attacked the southern end of the airfield while regiments of 39th and 79th Guard Divisions were ordered to advance outside the airfield boundary to the east and west, the artillery having instructions to maintain constant fire on the runways. We did not know the location of the exit doors to the underground hangars. Tanks with infantry support were therefore ordered to fire on the runway approaches to ensure that the aircraft remained immobilised underground.

The plan succeeded better than we could have hoped. From the evening of 25 April no more German aircraft took off and towards noon next day all of Tempelhof airport with its hangars, radio installations and main buildings was in our hands . . . The battle lasted three whole days and nights without pause. Gradually, the defended boundaries of the besieged city contracted and the defence became ever more desperate. Our infantry now had to engage in street-to-street fighting. Our artillery and mortar fire fell away to a minimum. Everybody was forced into the streets, reducing our advance to a snail's pace. From one street to the next, we had to find breaks in the thick walls of brick and stone, scramble over heaps of rubble and fallen masonry. The Nazis knew the end was near and destroyed houses and other buildings without regard to casualties amongst the civilian population, in order to increase our own casualty rate.

The strongest and most determined resistance was offered by the SS troops on the square in front of Kaiser Wilhelm Gedächtnis Church on the Kurfürstendamm. Historians should dedicate this square to their memory! It now lies in the British sector of Berlin.'*

Soviet Marshal Ivan Stepanovich Koniev completed the story with this entry from his diary beginning 26 April:

The battle for Berlin raged day and night. The Nazis had prepared the city for a long defence based on well-rigged defensive nests. The deeper our troops penetrated towards the heart of Berlin, the more bitter became the fighting. The massive stone houses with their thick walls were superbly suited for conversion into little fortresses: the windows and doors of many buildings had been reduced to narrow shooting-slits. Some of these reinforced buildings were grouped into defensive strong points whose sides were protected by barricades. The entire defensive system was organised very thoroughly. The enemy had massive quantities of Panzerfaust shoulder-fired anti-tank rockets, which were a feared weapon for our tanks in the street fighting.

The underground installations below the entire city, air-raid shelters, subway tunnels and the canal system also had an important role for the regrouping of their forces and the movement of supplies. The enemy used them to give us many very unpleasant surprises. It would often happen that, after capturing an enemy strongpoint, our troops would think that the action was concluded. Then suddenly enemy reconnaissance groups, a diversionary tactic or snipers would come up through the undergrounds shafts and resume the fighting from our rear. These skirmishes often put us into very difficult situations . . .

The advance of our troops into the heart of Berlin was hindered by a series of other circumstances. In the city centre, there were many steel-reinforced concrete bunkers. These had room for

* Vasily Chuikov, *Das Ende des Dritten Reiches*, Munich 1966, pp.163ff.

200–1,000 troops. We also came across five-storeyed bunkers thirty-six metres high with walls from one to three metres thick. These were invulnerable to field artillery. Generally there would be some flak artillery on the roof of these bunkers, which fired on our aircraft and also on our tanks and infantry below.* These bunkers were the principal strong points for the defence of inner Berlin. Besides these, the Germans had many MG nests in cupolas of steel-reinforced concrete. Whenever our soldiers came anywhere near them, our men were welcomed by a withering fire. There was an enormous amount of flak in Berlin, which played an especially important anti-tank role in the street fighting. Alongside the Panzerfaust, the flak guns caused our greatest losses in tanks: during Operation Berlin, the Nazis destroyed more than 800 tanks and SP guns, most of them during the fighting in the inner city.

In order to reduce our casualties, we found a simple but very effective method. We provided our tanks with a so-called protective screen of steel or iron plating. When the Panzerfaust went through the plating, it exploded in the empty space between the plating and the tank armour . . . The Volkssturm battalions in particular, that is to say the units made up mainly of older men or boys, were equipped with the Panzerfaust. These grenadiers, though lacking almost any military training and having little battle experience, were nevertheless dangerous opponents for our troops. The Panzerfaust was one of those weapons that lends a feeling of self-confidence to an untrained infantryman: he is scarcely a soldier, yet is capable of achieving a feat of arms.

I have to recognise that in general these Panzerfaust grenadiers fought very well to the end: they surrendered only when they saw no alternative. The same went also for the officers, although the old fighting spirit was gone. They had given up all hope. They held out doggedly and kept the fight going until they received the

---

* Koniev apparently means here the large flak towers at Humboldthain, Friedrichshain and the Zoo. (Author)

---

order to surrender. The Volkssturm men seemed to be possessed by a compulsion that I can most nearly describe as a hysterical death wish. These defenders of the Third Reich, among whom were many youths, believed and hoped to the last that a miracle would come.[*]

On the evening of 26 April as ordered, Colonel General Ritter von Greim reported in company with the intrepid Hanna Reitsch. He had been wounded during the flight. Reitsch reported:

Surprisingly the flight went smoothly until just before we got to Berlin. Nevertheless the minutes, as I watched them tick away on the luminous face of my watch, seemed short eternities. Never had I known such anxiety during a flight, so exposed were we to whatever dark fates might lurk to confront us. Suddenly – I suppose we were over the city outskirts – the pilot put the machine into a very steep dive and we roared towards the ground. Greater than the physical strain for me at this moment – I was lying head down – was the inner excitement, for I was certain that our aircraft had been hit and now I waited for us to impact the ground or explode. In fact, the pilot had dived to avoid Russian fighters, which had come to attack us: after a while I saw that he was pulling us out of the downwards plunge and shortly after he landed the machine on the airfield at Gatow.

We found the air-raid bunker housing the airfield command post from where Greim rang the Reich Chancellery. Eventually he got through with the greatest difficulty after an endless string of breaks in the connection. In response to his enquiry, Colonel von Below (Hitler's Luftwaffe adjutant) said that Hitler wanted to speak to Greim face to face at all costs but without saying why. Greim was also told that all access roads into the city were held by

---

[*] Gosztony, *Der Kampf um Berlin 1945*, pp.264ff., quoting Ivan Koniev, *Das Jahr 1945*, Berlin 1960.

the Russians, and in the inner city they had Anhalter station, the Knee, and parts of Bülow-Strasse and Potsdamer-Strasse. If this was the true situation, it appeared almost impossible for us to reach the Reich Chancellery, but Greim felt duty-bound to try to obey the order if at all possible. After some discussion, we decided to fly a Fieseler-Storch and land at the Brandenburg Gate. The first Storch was hit by artillery fire shortly before take-off. Not until six that evening was the second and last Storch ready to go. Greim decided to pilot it himself because I had no combat experience in flights over enemy-held territory. Before taking off, I stood behind his seat and reached over his left shoulder to confirm I could reach the gas lever and control stick in an emergency.

The machine lifted off beautifully and we hugged the ground. Below us the Wannsee glittered silver in the setting sun, a peaceful image of nature! I merely glanced at it, for I was fully on alert to the dangers that surrounded us. Now we were over Grunewald, skimming the tree tops to evade enemy fighters which roamed everywhere. Suddenly, from the ground and the shadows and the trees there began a hellish fire which I assumed was intended for us. I was right: below us swarmed Russians tanks and soldiers. I saw their faces clearly as they shot at us with everything they had: rifles, machine pistols, tank weapons. To the left and right of us, above and below, small destructive puffs of smoke and a fearsome din. I saw yellow-white flame flare up near the engine and heard Greim cry out immediately that he had been hit. A tank shell had gone through his right foot. Almost automatically, I reached over his shoulder for the gas lever and control stick and tried to keep the machine weaving. Greim had meanwhile lost consciousness and was slumped in his seat. Countless explosions still rent the air, so loud I could scarcely hear the engine. The aircraft was being hit time and again. With alarm, I saw fuel streaming out of the wing tanks both sides. I expected the aircraft to blow up at any moment and could not believe it did not do so. The Storch remained manoeuvrable, and I sustained no injury. I was concerned for Greim. He was conscious for brief periods, when he would attempt to regain control of the aircraft himself rather energetically, but the stick would always slip from his grasp.

We were coming near the radio tower. Smoke, dust and an acrid smell became ever thicker, but we seemed to have out-flown the shooting and were apparently now flying over German-held suburbs. I headed the aircraft for the radio tower, but visibility was poor. Now my training flights over Berlin came in useful. I did not need to orient my course from the ground, which in this predicament would have been dangerous, for I knew the compass course to the zoo flak bunker. The East–West axis with the Victory Column was to the left of it. I put the machine down right in front of the Brandenburg Gate with hardly a drop of fuel left in the tanks. The area was deserted. Uprooted trees, torn-off branches and concrete blocks were strewn everywhere, a fearful sight, no living thing to be seen. After a long struggle I managed to get the Colonel General, now returning to consciousness again, out of the machine: we had been spotted from the air and came under fire. Greim lay by the roadside. We waited in hope that a vehicle would pass by. Whether German or enemy was left to chance. Time dragged by. Artillery pounded the area nearby, nothing but an eerie wasteland. And then – I have no idea how long we had been waiting there – a German truck came by. We hailed it and were taken aboard.

We were driven through the Brandenburg Gate, down Unter den Linden, along Wilhelm-Strasse and turned into Voss-Strasse. What I saw on the way seemed like a parody when I remembered the proud buildings of former days. Nothing remained of them but rubble, ashes and an acrid smell of burning. We left the truck at the entrance to the Reich Chancellery air-raid shelter. SS guards took the Colonel General to the surgical room in the bunker where Dr Stumpfegger worked on the wound. After that we were taken

– Greim on a stretcher – two floors down into the Führer-bunker. On the stairway Frau Goebbels met us: it was the first time I had seen her in person; I recognised her from photographs. She stared briefly and wide-eyed at our small cortege as if unable to believe that people were still able to get here from outside. Then she fell tearfully into my arms.

In the Führer-bunker we met Adolf Hitler in the small vestibule-like corridor. He was very stooped, both his arms trembled and he had a glazed, distant look to his eyes. He greeted us in an almost flat voice. Greim made his report. Hitler listened calmly and attentively. When Greim had finished, Hitler grasped his hands and said, turning to me: 'You brave woman! There is still loyalty and courage in the world.' Then he explained why he had sent for Greim. He considered himself betrayed by Göring. Hitler showed Greim the telex in which Göring had set out his plans as successor: 'There is nothing left for me in the world, no disappointment, no breach of faith, no dishonour and no betrayal I have not experienced. I have had Göring arrested, relieved him of all his offices and expelled him from all organisations.' Then he named Greim as Göring's successor with immediate promotion to Field Marshal.

In the room it was quiet. I looked at the face of the new Field Marshal, impassive with tightly pressed lips. It was not difficult to guess what thoughts and feelings were running through his mind at this appointment. Commander-in-chief of a Luftwaffe which no longer existed! In this situation, the task for this man, whose concept of honour as an officer remained unchanged through the chaos and was above any personal considerations, could mean only one thing – he would experience the end of the Third Reich in the bunker! And that meant I would have to stay too.

The social circle was small. Besides Dr Goebbels and his wife, who had decided of their own free will to remain in Berlin with their children, I got to know Eva Braun. Later I also came across Martin Bormann, Secretary of State Naumann, Foreign Office liaison officer Hewel, Admiral Voss, Colonel von Below, General Krebs, General Burgdorf, Hitler's personal pilots Baur and Beetz, the female secretaries Frau Christian, Frau Junge and Fräulein Krüger, Dr Lorenz, SS-Gruppenführer Rattenhuber and SS-Gruppenführer Fegelein, who shortly before had married Eva Braun's sister. With the exception of Goebbels, those I have mentioned were accommodated in bunker rooms one floor higher. Hitler, Eva Braun, Goebbels and Stumpfegger lodged in the lowest floor of the bunker.

Whenever I was not needed to nurse Field Marshal von Greim, I devoted myself to the Goebbels children. Shortly after meeting Hitler, Frau Goebbels had invited me to her room one floor higher, to clean the dust and filth from myself. When I entered the room I found myself looking at six beautiful faces of children aged from four to twelve years, who viewed me from their tiered bunk beds with lively curiosity. That I could fly an aircraft immediately opened the door wide on their childish fantasies and whilst I – still in turmoil after my recent experiences – washed, they chattered and asked me questions all at once, forcing me to enter their colourful world whether I wanted to or not. From then on, I had to spend each mealtime with them and tell them about the foreign countries and people I had seen, about my flights, or tell them fairy stories. Each child delighted in her natural, clever and private way. The sisterly love between the five girls had something captivating about it. When one of them was isolated in a neighbouring room with croup, from time to time I would have to break off my stories so that one of the girls could inform their sibling of the next part of the story. I taught them to sing as a choir and to yodel correctly the Tyrolean way, which they picked up very quickly. The thunder and crash of the shelling did not unnerve them, for it had been explained that this was how 'Uncle Führer' would beat the enemy. When the youngest once became anxious, she was quickly comforted by her sisters. This peaceful scenario, which remained unchanged while the tension grew hourly and rose towards the almost intolerable, caused me almost the greatest inner suffering I had ever had to carry. Often it seemed scarcely tolerable. 'Tomorrow morning, if God wills it, you will be awoken,' I used to sing with the children every night before they fell asleep. Would they be awoken?

The other bunker dwellers were composed and resigned, but I only met them on chance occasions. On the first night I spent in the bunker, 26 April, the Russians were finally close enough to shell the Reich Chancellery. An incessant artillery barrage drummed out with increasing violence. Beneath the thunder and crash of the hits, the plaster flaked from the walls even of these lowest floors. Sleep was impossible. Everybody was in a state of readiness. I did not doubt that the end was approaching: everybody sensed it. Recognition of this fact had a strange effect on all the occupants, giving rise to hopes that were basically irrational. The close circle around Hitler lived in hope of salvation. This hope was nourished by rumours and reports reaching the bunker from time to time. These created ideas that in view of the situation presented a distorted picture of reality. This hope included the relief of Berlin. The impression was specially strong for those who – like ourselves – came from outside. Although we were all crammed together down there and perhaps in a few hours we would share the fate of the permanent inhabitants of the bunker, it was as if a partition divided off Greim and myself from them. This inner distancing became greater the more desperate the situation became.

On the two days following (27 and 28 April) nothing happened to change the situation fundamentally. The hours passed in anxious waiting: occasionally new hope was whipped up and gave birth to illusions, or bad news came and spread through the bunker like wildfire. Fegelein – liaison officer between Himmler and Hitler since 1 January 1944 and Eva Braun's brother-in-law – was sentenced to be shot by firing squad on Hitler's order for desertion. In such moments it seemed to me that the floor would cave in.

The violence of the attacks on the Reich Chancellery increased hourly. There was no doubt: the Russians were edging ever closer. We had given up all hope of ever seeing daylight again. The report that a Ju 52 had landed on the Axis to bring Greim and myself out of Berlin seemed like a miracle. Rudel also rang from Rechlin to offer his help but Greim declined. On the second day of our stay in the bunker, Hitler had sent for me. When I saw him in his sitting room, a shade paler, more stooped, his face discoloured with age, he gave me two phials of poison so that – as he said – Greim and I should have the freedom of choice at any time. He also explained that he and Eva Braun would voluntarily depart this life once there was no further hope that General Wenck could relieve Berlin. Even if Wenck's Army could have fulfilled his hopes, it was my impression however that he did not have the strength to go on. He turned down flat all opportunities still available to save himself offered by the Ju 52 and Ar 96 aircraft standing on the East–West axis. All that kept him alive was his belief that his being in Berlin was the last spur to his soldiers.

On the night of 28 April one barrage of fire followed another, a hurricane of explosives rained down on the Reich Chancellery. According to one rumour, the Russians had reached the far end of Wilhelm-Strasse and were also up to Potsdamer Platz. Shortly before midnight, Hitler came unexpectedly to Greim's sickbed. Chalk-white in the face, it seemed to me the picture of a life that had already been extinguished. In his hand he held a signal and a map. Turning to Greim he said: 'Now even Himmler has betrayed me. Both of you must leave the bunker as quickly as possible. I have read a report that the Russians will attempt to storm the Reich Chancellery during the course of the morning.' He unfolded the map. 'If we succeed in bombing and destroying these assembly points on the access roads to the Reich Chancellery, we can win at least twenty-four hours more and give General Wenck the chance of breaking through to us. German artillery has been heard at Potsdam.' He then said that an Arado 96 had managed a landing on the East–West axis, and was at our disposal.

I had no understanding of military matters. It was beyond me how one could still sensibly talk at this juncture of a liberation. I thought of the scenes we had observed in recent weeks everywhere in Germany, of streets and highways filled to overflowing with the fleeing populace, troops flooding back, of the hail of bombs during the nights, the endless artillery fire to which the Reich Chancellery had been subjected for days – to my way of thinking Wenck's Army could not help mend all this.

Yet the world of illusion was not quite dead. In tears, Frau Goebbels made me promise to leave no stone unturned in trying to bring salvation. The moral responsibility for that was Greim's. We got ourselves ready. I found Hitler in the situation conference room and took my leave of him with a brief handshake. I could find nothing to say to him, while he muttered softly: 'God protect you!'. Frau Goebbels, whom I had come to know in those few days as a woman of exemplary composure, gave me a letter for her son by her first marriage. Her children were sleeping. How I would have loved to have seen them just once more. I bade the others goodbye without speaking.

Colonel von Below accompanied Greim, struggling on crutches, and myself up to the open. The higher we came the more acrid was the smell of burning and smouldering, the worse the dust in the air from the wall plaster. There was a pause in the shelling. As we emerged into Voss-Strasse the sky was a peculiar red-yellow sea of flame. A panzer took us aboard. Now began an eerie ride over the rubble of Voss-Strasse. A street it was no longer. The whistle of the shells and the crash of the hits filled the air, shook the ground; fire and smoke rose upwards. Worse than all this was the uncertainty whether we might be straying into Russian-held territory.

We passed the corner of Voss-Strasse/Hermann Göring-Strasse without incident and breathed a sigh of relief. Next we reached the zoo, and then the flight control centre at the Victory Column, which was still in German hands. The Axis itself was under constant fire. The Ar 96 stood in an anti-shrapnel shelter. Under these circumstances it had been an outstanding feat to land the aircraft here. It was the same pilot who had flown us to Gatow. Now he had to fly the aircraft out with two passengers with only a seat for one.

Scouts reported that the Axis was clear of shell craters for 400 metres. That could change at any moment. In any case we would need some luck at take-off. The long fingers of enemy searchlights swept the Axis unceasingly, but we managed to get up unseen and headed for the Brandenburg Gate. The victory chariot was a black silhouette in the searchlight beams. We flew above it and away. The enemy spotted us and fired tracer. The air seemed full of it.

At about 1,700 metres altitude the pilot found some cloud and flew into it. Overhead the sky was bright and clear. We headed for Rechlin. The silver gleam of the Brandenburg Lakes contrasted with the red glare from the burning villages everywhere, putting an ornamental edge on the scene of war and destruction. We landed at Rechlin at three in the morning to be greeted in silence by those of the Luftwaffe command staff still there. Frozen, dead tired and shocked inwardly by all we had experienced, we got out of the machine and trod solid ground once more.[*]

On 27 April, the Twelfth Army reached Ferch south of Potsdam. The 20,000 men under General Reimann trapped in the cauldron and who had abandoned hope broke out to join up jubilantly with Wenck's divisions. The news sped like an electric current through those parts of Berlin still in German hands: 'Wenck, Wenck, Wenck!' A crazy hope blossomed. Not only the civilian population

* Hanna Reitsch, *Fliegen mein Leben*, Stuttgart 1951, p.295ff. Published in English as *The Sky My Kingdom*, London 1955.

but General Weidling's men fighting with a valour beyond the call of duty were filled with new confidence. The 40,000 exhausted men of the Ninth Army, surrounded alongside 10,000 civilians, mostly women and children, sighed with relief. Wenck signalled the order to Theodor Busse to break out. The battle groups hesitated, then attacked the encirclement with a courage born of despair. It gave way. Women and children carried weapons and ammunition for their soldiers.

The Red Army was not prepared to be deprived of its prey. Marshall Zhukov threw all his available forces against the Twelfth Army. Although 30,000 men of the Ninth Army and many thousands of civilians reached the Twelfth Army lines, there was no more talk of relieving Berlin. In the face of the overwhelming numerical superiority of the Red Army, General Wenck could simply go no further. The last hope evaporated.

The BBC announced officially at 1355 hrs on 28 April 1945 that Heinrich Himmler had offered the Western Allies the unconditional surrender of the Reich. The Allies had replied that they would only accept the capitulation in common with the Soviet Union. Hitler was stupefied. After Göring, this attempt to supersede him as Head of State hit him hard. He had had no suspicion that for months the Reichsführer-SS had been under the spell of his espionage chief Walter Schellenberg.

Schellenberg had long been playing a double game with the West. In February 1945 he had brought together Himmler and Folke Count Bernadotte, vice-president of the Swedish Red Cross, who was negotiating for the release of Norwegian and Danish POWs. Secret talks between them were held at Hohenlychen on 19 February 1945. SS-Brigadeführer* Hermann Fegelein, Himmler's liaison officer to Hitler at FHQ, had the job of sounding out Hitler for his opinion on these talks with Bernadotte. Hitler responded

---

* Correctly SS-Gruppenführer. (TN)

brusquely: 'In total war one can achieve nothing with an idiot like that.'*

At Hohenlychen, only the POWs were discussed. Himmler agreed to their being centralised in northwest Germany. Schellenberg kept on at Himmler, suggesting finally that he should request Bernadotte to fly to see Eisenhower in order to pass him Himmler's offer of capitulation. Himmler declined, mentioning his oath of loyalty from which he could not deviate as Reichsführer-SS. Schellenberg, who worked openly for the British secret service after the war to the extent that they even placed a villa on Lake Como at his disposal, would not be brushed aside so easily.

On 22 April,† Himmler, Schellenberg and Bernadotte met again at Hohenlychen. This conversation also led nowhere but was continued at Lübeck the following evening when Himmler told Bernadotte:

> 'We Germans must declare ourselves vanquished to the Western Powers, and in order to spare further bloodshed I request you to deliver this declaration to General Eisenhower through the Swedish government. To capitulate to the Russians, however, is impossible for us Germans and quite especially for me personally. We will fight on against them until the Western Powers replace the German front.' Himmler then claimed that he was empowered to negotiate because it could only be a question of two to three days before Hitler gave up his life. Alive he would never surrender to the Bolshevists, against whom he would continue the fight to the last man.'‡

On 26 April, Himmler and Schellenberg were informed by Count Levenhaupt of the Swedish consulate at Flensburg that the Allies

---

* Walter Schellenberg, *Memoiren*, Cologne 1956, p.354.
† Author says February must be error. (TN)
‡ Schellenberg, *Memoiren*, p.363.

had declined to consider Himmler's offer. If it was incredibly naive of Göring to think that London and Washington would recognise him as a negotiating partner, then Himmler's illusion was utterly incomprehensible. He was linked inseparably to the persecution of the Jews and nobody, certainly not the United States and Great Britain, would negotiate with him. That was certain from the outset. That he succumbed to Schellenberg's whispers speaks for the panic to which he was prey, and of which Joachim Fest later wrote: 'Other than Göring, Ribbentrop or Ley, he not only simply carried out Hitler's orders, but thought them through to their conclusion and in contrast to Rosenberg had the power to make them reality: that confirms his rank and status in the hierarchy of the Third Reich.'*

Joachim Fest, who knows that historical research has still failed to come up with a written order from Hitler to exterminate the Jews, likes to gloss over this fact and links Himmler's undoubted complicity in the extermination programme indirectly to Hitler. That Himmler, who was inseparably part of the order to exterminate the Jews, could have expected a merciful reception from the United States is a preposterous idea.

Göring dusted himself down before the Nuremberg Trials, and by his manly composure attempted to make up for what he undoubtedly lacked as leader of the Luftwaffe, but to no avail, for the judges had already decided beforehand to hang him: and according to official Allied reports Himmler took poison immediately the British saw through his thin disguise as a Wehrmacht sergeant. In his political testament, Hitler expelled both from the Party.

In Berlin, the situation was deteriorating rapidly. Neither Busse nor Heinrici were obeying Hitler's orders. Busse was leading the remnants of his army towards the Americans, while Heinrici, like

* Bradley Smith & Agnes Peterson (eds), *Heinrich Himmler – Geheimreden 1933 bis 1945*, Frankfurt 1974, with an introduction by Joachim Fest, p.14.

General von Manteuffel, was also marching his troops through Mecklenburg towards the Western Allies.*

The extent to which Hermann Fegelein, Himmler's liaison officer to Hitler, was involved in Himmler's secret negotiations is not known. He had disappeared from the bunker on 26 April without anybody thinking that anything was amiss. He then phoned Eva Braun, his sister-in-law, urging her to leave Hitler and flee Berlin with him. She declined indignantly and demanded that Fegelein return to the bunker at once. Shortly after, Hitler needed to consult Fegelein on a routine matter. He could not be found, although next day SS-Brigadeführer Rattenhuber contacted him by telephone at his private flat on Bleibtreu-Strasse. Fegelein, unnerved, stated that he was drunk and could not come. SS-Obersturmbannführer Helmut Frick was sent to persuade Fegelein to return, but failed to convince him and finally Rattenhuber sent the RSD heavy brigade to bring him in. SS-Standartenführer Peter Högl found Fegelein in civilian clothing and in the company of a lady suspected to be a British agent.† A trunk packed with jewellery, gold bars, 105,725 Reichsmarks and 3,186 Swiss francs was found. Fegelein was taken back to the Führer-bunker with the trunk: the lady was allowed to go.

Hitler was beside himself with rage about the desertion and ordered Fegelein to be court martialled. He was taken to Mohnke's command post but was returned to the Führer-bunker as being unfit to stand trial by reason of drunkenness. Once sober, he was interrogated on 28 April by Gestapo chief Heinrich Müller. Around midday the same day the radio broadcast news of Himmler's failed attempt to capitulate to the Western Powers. Hitler was convinced that Fegelein was fully implicated in the plot, and shortly before eleven that night he was shot for treason by an RSD firing squad

---

* Irving, *Hitler und Seine Feldherren*, pp.726f.

† Bahnsen & O'Donnell, *Die Katakombe*, p.203. This version of events is obviously markedly different from Kempka's account.

in the Ehrenhof courtyard at the Reich Chancellery. A little later, Hitler married Eva Braun.

On 29 April the plight of the defenders of Berlin deteriorated. The Red Army was throwing ever more troops and materials against the last exhausted but tenacious German fighting groups. At this time a monstrous false legend was created. Rittmeister Gerhard Boldt, one of General Krebs's officers, had left the Führer-bunker in an attempt to contact Wenck and had deserted. Boldt broadcast the following version:

> Without regard to the hungry, thirsty and the dying in Berlin, he (Hitler) wants to spin out the battle. And now comes the most inhumane of his orders. Because the Russians had repeatedly rolled up our front by attacking through the subway and tramway tunnels to our rear, he ordered the locks of the Spree to be opened to flood the tunnels south of the Reich Chancellery. Thousands of wounded were being tended there. Human life means nothing to him. They all drowned miserably.[*]

This fairy tale, included by Cornelius Ryan in his book *The Last Battle*[†] with no prior attempt to verify it, supplied the fuel for years to keep the untrue version of history current. Hitler's adjutant SS-Sturmbannführer Otto Günsche, at Hitler's side day and night throughout that tragic period, was present at all situation conferences and passed on all of Hitler's orders. He declared:

> It is a fact that on one occasion during a situation conference somebody suggested flooding the subway tunnels. This idea was rejected immediately, because there were numerous dressing stations in the tunnels and thousands of Berliners sheltered there

---

[*] Gerhard Boldt, *Die letzten Tage der Reichskanzlei*, Zurich 1948, pp.76f.

[†] Cornelius Ryan, *Der Letzte Kampf*, Stuttgart 1966. Published in English as *The Last Battle*, London 1966.

from Soviet shells and bombs. Hitler never gave such an order and therefore the tunnels were never flooded. Whoever says the contrary is a liar.[*]

SS-Brigadeführer Wilhelm Mohnke, who as citadel commandant was present at all conferences in the Führer-bunker at this time, stated as follows:

'On 25 or 26 April after a situation conference (attended by Hitler, Goebbels, Bormann, Krebs and myself) there was a discussion about what could be done to improve the security of the citadel. A question was asked whether it would be possible for Soviet troops to infiltrate the inner city through the subway and tramway tunnels and what countermeasures could be taken, including flooding the tunnels. That same day, Goebbels as defence commissioner consulted subway and tramway experts, who told him that if the subway network was to be blown up this would increase the water level by between sixty and ninety centimetres. It was confirmed expressly that the subway and tramway tunnels were being inhabited by the population of Berlin to such an extent that a future evacuation would not be possible. For these two reasons, the idea of flooding the tunnels was rejected. The Reich Chancellery never issued such an order.'[†]

The final word on this foul legend must rest with Senate adviser R. Fritz Kraft, who was the responsible authority for the Berlin subway for years and supervised the renovation work on it after the war:

---

[*] Affidavit dated 3 July 1975, from Otto Günsche, in author's possession.

[†] Written declaration 2 August 1975, from Wilhelm Mohnke, in author's possession.

Fritz Kraft can testify that thousands of drowned persons in the underground tunnels are an invention to replace the true facts, which lack drama. He knows of three ways in which water entered:

1. A bomb hit cracked the roof of the subway tunnel below the Spree between Märkisches Museum and Kloster-Strasse without passing through it.
2. An explosion occurred in the tramway tunnel below the Landwehr Canal; although water poured in at the breach, it dispersed immediately. Nobody drowned.
3. Because of the failure of ground-water pumps, which depended on the electric grid, superficial flooding occurred here and there.

Senate adviser Kraft terminated his statement with the observation that over the course of the years, journalists who asked him about the events of those times always lost interest when he related the true facts.*

---

* Erich Kuby, *Die Russen in Berlin*, Munich 1980, pp.163f.

Appendix 2

The Break-out from the Citadel

THE SPECTRE OF DEATH enveloped the whole Führer-bunker. SS-Brigadeführer Mohnke and his chief of staff Klingemeier began separating people into groups in preparation for the armed break-out. The following had definitely decided to go: Martin Bormann, who intended to join Admiral Dönitz at Flensburg; Secretary of State Dr Werner Naumann; SS-Brigadeführer Johann Rattenhuber; SS-Brigadeführer Jürgen Ziegler; SS-Standartenführer Peter Högl, head of the RSD at FHQ; Hitler's last physician Dr Ludwig Stumpfegger; Oberstarzt Dr Ernst Schenck; Goebbels's adjutant Günther Schwägermann; Hitler's adjutant SS-Sturmbannführer Otto Günsche; Hitler's chief pilot SS-Obergruppenführer Flugkapitän Hans Baur; Dönitz's representative Vizeadmiral Hans Voss; Ribbentrop's representative Walter Hewel; Hitler's principal manservant SS-Hauptsturmführer Heinz Linge; Hitler's remaining secretaries Trudl Junge and Gerda Christian; Hitler's dietician-cook Konstanze Manziarly; Bormann's secretary Elsa Krüger; and head of the FHQ vehicle pool, Hitler's chauffeur SS-Obersturmbannführer Erich Kempka. The civilians, particularly the women, presented a problem that had to be taken into account.

Shortly before eight on the evening of 1 May 1945 the following order was issued to all command posts of fighting units still offering resistance to the Russians in the vicinity of the Reich Chancellery:

The Führer is dead. All persons are released from their oath of allegiance to him. The city will go to the Russians at two o'clock tomorrow afternoon, the enemy has insisted on unconditional surrender. What happens after the capitulation is therefore wholly dependent on their whim.

A Freikorps led by the last commander of *Leibstandarte Adolf Hitler,* and composed of able volunteers from all units, is being formed immediately and will break out tonight. The operation will attempt to penetrate the encirclement to create corridors for the passage of wounded and civilians using two spearheads to Stettiner Bahnhof and Friedrich-Strasse to the north and northwest. It is uncertain and probably doubtful that our forces will be strong enough for this purpose. We are armed only with infantry weapons, while the enemy system of cordons is constructed in depth. In the most favourable circumstances, we can expect to be engaged in fighting for eighteen hours before we reach the city limits.

Once the battle begins, we will not take seriously wounded Freikorps fighters with us. In such a situation, whoever does not wish to fall into enemy hands will be given the *coup de grâce.* The objective of all units and men who succeed in breaking out is to link up with our forces still fighting in the north. We know nothing of their situation; we have had no contact with them for forty-eight hours.

Admiral Dönitz has been appointed Reich President, his orders are binding. The Freikorps units will assemble at the places ordered by 2000 hrs and will move from there into their waiting positions.*

That night feverish anticipation gripped everybody. In the cellars and ruins of dwellings the last assault troops gathered for the attempt to fight through to the west. The groups from the Führer-bunker formed part of them. Mohnke had planned for ten break-out

---

* Gosztony, *Der Kampf um Berlin 1945,* p.382.

groups. He would lead the first himself, Rattenhuber the second, Naumann the third. The break-out would begin at 2300 hrs with half-hourly intervals between groups. The route was northwest through Wedding to Schwerin, where all those who had made it would regroup to join up with Dönitz at Plön.

The Mohnke–Klingemeier–Günsche group left the bunker on time with twenty men and four women. Initially they made good progress and, eluding detection by the Red Army, reached the subway station at Wilhelms-Platz from where they headed down the tunnel towards Stadtmitte station. They had no contact with other groups since they lacked radios. At 0100 on 2 May they came to an iron doorway, which sealed the tunnel. Before it stood two uniformed officials of the Berlin transport board, who refused to open the door since it was required to be kept closed at night by the regulations. The train service had been suspended for some weeks. Now occurred the most inexplicable event in the entire drama. Instead of drawing his pistol and forcing the officials to open the door, Mohnke, proven hero of many campaigns and decorated with the Knights Cross, accepted the situation and led his group, to which hundreds of other refugees had attached themselves, along a new route over the Spree left of Weidendammer Bridge. This brought them back to Friedrich-Strasse.[*]

From there, Mohnke's group had to scramble over the rubble between the Spree and Invaliden-Strasse. Suddenly they heard the sound of heavy firing from the direction of Weidendammer Bridge. This was Kempka's group which had run into a Soviet cordon. In this skirmish, in which the last panzers of SS-Division *Nordland* were involved, Kempka was injured, as described in his own account earlier in this volume, and he lost consciousness temporarily.

When this occurred, Kempka was in contact with Bormann, Naumann, Schwägermann, Stumpfegger, Hitler's second

---

[*] Bahnsen & O'Donnell, *Die Katakombe*, p.264.

personal pilot Georg Beetz and Artur Axmann, who had broken out with another group and had also finished up at Weidendammer Bridge.*

When Kempka regained consciousness, he found the mortally wounded Beetz, whom he put on a cart and placed in the care of Frau Käthe Häusermann (who was on the staff of Dr Blaschke, Hitler's dentist). Subsequently Kempka was helped to escape to the west, as was Naumann and Axmann.

From this moment, nothing more was known of the fate of Martin Bormann. Axmann, who had crossed the area around Lehrter station with his adjutant Günter Weltzin, stated that he had seen Bormann dead. He reported:

> We came across the bodies of Martin Bormann and his companion Dr Stumpfegger. They lay close together without movement. I bent over them; I saw their faces. I found no evidence of a wound. At first I thought they were unconscious or sleeping, but they were not breathing. I assumed at the time and am more certain of it today that they had taken poison. We did not stay longer to check for a pulse and so on. In immediate danger as we were, we had no interest in gathering evidence for future historical debate. We resumed our course. It was still dark, very wet and cold. As I recall, first light was half an hour later, when we got to Wedding.†

Axmann made this statement in December 1945 after being detained by the Americans in Bavaria. Nobody believed what he said. Once everybody accepted Hitler's death and the Berchtesgaden court had declared him officially dead on 25 October 1956, historians began to follow the Bormann trail on the hypothesis that he was living somewhere under an alias and biding his time. Biding it for what,

---

* John Toland, *Das Finale*, Bergisch Gladbach 1978, p.528. Published in English as *The Last 100 Days*, London 1965.

† Bahnsen & O'Donnell, *Die Katakombe*, p.294.

nobody knew. While the missing Bormann breathed his last in an unmarked grave near the Lehrter station he became the quarry of Simon Wiesenthal, Ladislas Farago and other researchers – supposedly he was living in Arabia advising on the struggle against Israel; owning a great plantation somewhere in South America; or spying for the Soviets.

The background to the latter idea was grotesque. The survivors of the 20 July 1944 plot and their friends needed to divert attention from their accomplices and so presented Bormann as the not yet identified arch-traitor 'Werther'. The most lamentable role in this scheme was played by Reinhard Gehlen, when he stated mysteriously in his otherwise very interesting book *Der Dienst*:

At this point I want to break my long silence about a secret matter – most carefully guarded by the Soviets – which is the key to one of their greatest riddles of the century. It is the fateful role that Martin Bormann, Hitler's closest confidant, played in the latter years of the war and subsequently.

As the most prominent informer and adviser to the Soviets, he was working for the enemy from the beginning of the Russian campaign. Independently of each other (i.e. Admiral Canaris and Gehlen) we discovered that Bormann had the only unmonitored radio post. We were in agreement that a planned supervision of the most powerful man in the National Socialist hierarchy after Hitler was as good as out of the question. Any careless slip would have meant the end of the investigation and also of ourselves. Canaris told me his reasons for suspecting Bormann's traitorous activities, how he confirmed them and what he assumed. He did not exclude the possibility that Bormann was being blackmailed, but saw the probable motivation grounded in the man's boundless vanity and complexes towards his environment, and his ultimate aim to take over from Hitler one day. How skilfully Bormann brought his great rivals Göring and Goebbels alternatively into discredit with Hitler is now well known to us.

My own discoveries were not made known until after 1946, when I had the opportunity to investigate the mysterious circumstance of Bormann's escape from Hitler's bunker in Berlin and his disappearance. The allegations, often repeated in the international press, that Bormann is living in an impenetrable primeval forest between Paraguay and Argentina protected by heavily armed bodyguards has no foundation in fact. Two reliable sources convinced me in the 1950s that Bormann was living in perfect safety in the Soviet Union. The former Reichsleiter crossed over to the Red Army when Berlin was occupied and died in Russia.[*]

The fanciful Bormann legend died in 1973, when comparison of his dental records with a skull found in Berlin confirmed that Martin Bormann and Hitler' physician Dr Ludwig Stumpfegger died together on 2 May 1945. General Reinhard Gehlen does not come out of this affair well, for it was he who gave the Bormann hoax its credibility. In September 1971, he stated to the Frankfurt examining magistrate Horst von Glasenapp at Starnberg court that in 1946 or 1947 'one of his contact men' had seen a film report in the GDR (German Democratic Republic) weekly newsreel *Augenzeuge* about a sporting event in Moscow and picked out Bormann as the camera scanned the crowd. Gehlen declined to make this statement on oath, however.[†]

Thus the attempts to saddle Bormann with the role of the arch-traitor 'Werther' during the National Socialist period came to nothing. Nevertheless investigator Ladislas Farago published a factual account entitled *Scheintot* (seemingly dead) in which he claimed to have personally seen Bormann in South America. This kind of *Boy's Own* literature is not worthy of serious challenge.

---

[*] Reinhard Gehlen, *Der Dienst*, Munich 1971, pp.48f.

[†] *Der Spiegel*, No. 47/1971.

The same cloak-and-dagger atmosphere surrounded the disappearance of the former Gestapo chief Heinrich Müller, although he excited less interest than Bormann. It was alleged repeatedly that in 1945 Müller had been in the pay of the Kremlin, had been 'sighted' in the Soviet zone of Germany, even in Albania. This fable was cooked up by Walter Schellenberg, former head of Amt VI (Overseas) at SS-RSHA, and his colleagues. In office, Müller and Schellenberg were rivals and arch-enemies. After Müller disappeared in Berlin and Schellenberg joined the British, Schellenberg kept the old rivalry alive and let his adversary 'have the last say'.

Walter Hagen, a former close associate of Schellenberg, revealed in 1950:

It is even alleged by acquaintances of Müller that he was in contact with the Soviets at the end of 1944 and went over to them after the collapse. This version is not fantasy. The Gestapo had a section which kept the radio sets of captured Soviet agents operational. False information was thus supplied to the Soviets. The technical term for this was 'radio games'. There were about 300 in 1944. It is not out of the question that Müller had trusted staff using this set-up in the Gestapo section concerned, which contacted the Soviets before the capitulation with true reports, and it is possible that Müller changed sides and offered his services to the Soviets. There are reports from the GDR, so far impossible to verify, in which former Gestapo officials are said to have been 'retrained' in Russia.

As Gestapo head, Müller followed his orders faithfully in persecution of Communism, and he is responsible for having had put to death in concentration camps thousands of Communists working from belief in their cause and for a world union of Soviet states. From other cases, we know that the Bolshevists had no scruples about giving pardons to people they could use (even

short term), and they could use Müller. A man who for years
had been the head of the Gestapo, a force that during the years
of German expansion controlled most of mainland Europe, could
offer the Russians something uncommonly valuable: his wealth
of knowledge. Müller was known for his phenomenal memory:
he knew the names of every German agent in the world by heart.
There is certainly no police expert with such extensive personal
knowledge and a similarly deep insight into political affairs,
knowledge that even today (1950) is of significance. Therefore
it is not unthinkable that Müller is working for the Russians.
Admittedly there is no proof of it, at least not at present, but what
is certain is that after Hitler's death he disappeared from the Reich
Chancellery with his close friend Scholz, and neither was ever
heard of again.[*]

Flugkapitän Hans Baur recounted to American author O'Donnell
his last conversation with Heinrich Müller before the break-out
from the bunker:

Whoever knew his name feared him, even though he was never
as powerful as Himmler or Kaltenbrunner. To my knowledge
there is nothing mysterious about Müller's fate, or at least not up
to the evening of 1 May 1945. About one hour before the time to
go, shortly after dusk, I met him in the Reich Chancellery bunker;
we had a conversation during a lull in the firing. I think Müller
had come here to attach himself to one of the groups breaking out,
but to my enquiry he replied: 'Baur, my friend, I am a realist and
I know when the end has come. I can imagine pretty well how
the Russians would treat the chief of the Gestapo if they got their
hands on him, I have no illusions about that. No, I shall stay here
and use my pistol once the game is up, late this evening I think.'

* Walter Hagen, *Die Geheime Front*, Vienna 1950, pp.73ff.

Though I was very much opposed to the constant suicides of recent days, I did not try to persuade him against it. He knew more about Russian methods than all of us put together.[*]

Quite apart from these myths and fantasies about Müller and Bormann, the idea that the Bolsheviks had any use for Party bosses or SS people is absurd. Even if the Kremlin had wanted the bulk of the Party members in 1945, they would certainly not have wanted Bormann, who was hated by everybody at the upper levels. As the Red Army murdered, plundered and raped its way across central Germany, the Soviet NKVD threw hundreds of thousands of former Party members, officials, soldiers and police into concentration camps run by the Soviets on German soil. The death toll of those who did not survive beatings and starvation in these exceeded 90,000.[†] If the Soviets had kept their criminal army in check, if they had wanted to retain Germany as an entity, if they had declared a general amnesty, at least for the mass of the functionaries and NSDAP members without influence, the German masses would have gone over to them in droves.

Particularly amongst the Americans and British, numerous Jewish emigrants delighted in exacting a vicarious revenge: Germans soldiers on the Elbe and in Upper Austria in the hands of the Western Allies were passed over to the Russians if they had been facing them at the end, and they saw how the British and Americans returned Cossacks, Tartars and Caucasians to the Red hangmen for having fought for Germany. No, the Soviets did not want the German people!

---

[*] Bahnsen & O'Donnell, *Die Katakombe,* p.285.

[†] The author lists camps at: Oppeln, Troost/Gross-Strehlitz (Upper Silesia), Graudenz (West Prussia), Posen, Landsberg/Warthe, Frankfurt/Oder, Weesow/ Werneuchen, Berlin-Hohenschönhausen, Ketschendorf/Fürstenwalde, Jamlitz, Neubrandenburg, Mühlberg, Buchenwald, Torgau, Sachsenhausen and Bautzen.

The German volunteers were flown on 2 May 1945 direct from Moscow to Berlin in a military aircraft: Walter Ulbricht, Richard Gyptner, Otto Winzer, Gustav Gundlach, Fritz Erpenbeck, Karl Maron, Wolfgang Leonhard and associates. They set about creating a Communist administration immediately. When they needed additional police and army units, they called upon their human reserves in the 'National Committee for a Free Germany' and the 'League of German Officers'. Only a sick mind could imagine friendly contacts between leading National Socialists and Communists. National Socialism had been the only political force to seriously challenge the existence of Communism.

Flugkapitän Hans Baur failed in his attempt to break out to freedom. He finished up seriously wounded.

When I ran back, it was already dawn. The wild running did for me. As we ran along the Spree Canal to Wilhelm-Strasse bridge, accurate fire forced us to retire. Then along the tram tracks – Russian fire from the Reichstag building – we made a new attempt to shelter in tramway embankment from Lehrter station to the Charité. Accurate and scattered fire claimed victims. Close to Lehrter station we went through a courtyard. As we established later, Russian infantry with machine pistols had the entrance covered. We ran into bursts of fire. A terrible blow to both legs floored me.

I must have cried out in pain. Somebody grabbed me and dragged me into a burning house whose whole front facade had been blown away. My badly damaged leg was splinted with strips of wood and cardboard. The wound to the other leg, a clean shot through, was dressed. In the excitement I had not noticed other wounds to my chest and hand.

The cellar was on fire. The ground on which I was laid got ever hotter. I had my pistol close by. I intended to shoot myself with it should flames trap me. The entrance to the house remained under fire. Ricochets rebounded off the walls. Somewhere nearby wounded men were crying for help. After about four hours, these cries attracted the attention of a Russian, who turned up with three wounded German prisoners. From him I heard for the first time the term *'Uri-uri'* (wristwatch) which later became so familiar. When he saw my pistol he waved his white flag, but once sure I was beyond fighting his interest returned to my *Uri-uri*. He liked the look of it very much. The aviator's watch – fitted with every imaginable extra – appealed to him, being far superior to the other ten or so timepieces in his collection. I could tell this from his happy expression and the joyful utterance *'karosh, karosh!'*. He also liked my Walther PPK. Then he ordered a bed to be dismantled and I was carried on a stretcher all the way to Invaliden-Strasse.

At the assembly point were fifty to sixty German soldiers. A police officer who spoke Russian was helping the Soviets take down personal details. When I gave my rank as Lieutenant General he looked disconcerted. I was wearing a camouflage jacket and until then nobody had given me a second look. Now there was movement. The policeman ran to the Russians immediately. After a short while, a Russian colonel came over and asked me to sign my name on a blank piece of paper. Obviously I refused. The colonel then explained that he required generals' signatures to append to a proclamation calling on German soldiers to surrender. I replied that I had been Hitler's chief pilot and was not involved in military affairs. The defence of Berlin was the responsibility of General Weidling, to whom he should apply. After threats got him nowhere, he had me dragged off into an empty room and laid on a table. Weak through loss of blood I had the shivers. After about two hours, some Russians took me to my first interrogation.*

* Hans Baur, *Ich Flog Mächtige der Welt*, Oldendorf 1973, pp.278ff. Published in English as *Hitler's Pilot*, London 1958.

The Panzer Corps *Grossdeutschland* chronicler portrayed the break-out of the men of the unit thus:

Despatch riders sped through the streets of Berlin to the sector commanders bearing orders to break off contact with the enemy and break out in small groups. At 2300 hrs on 1 May 1945 Major Lehnhoff ordered his units of Guard Regiment *Grossdeutschland* to Kastanien Allee to attempt the break-out to the west through Rathenow. The remaining vehicles were fully fuelled, millions of Reichsmarks distributed amongst the men, the last rations consumed, and they set off. At Schönhauser-Allee station the break-out through the Russian lines succeeded, despite heavy losses from tank fire and Stalin organs.* Lehnhoff broke out of the city to Oranienburg with five panzers and sixty-eight men led by Lieutenant Hempel. Here the panzers were destroyed for lack of fuel. The men split up into four groups and headed for the Elbe and Schleswig-Holstein, while Lieutenant Kralack and Captain Hauck remained in Berlin. They were probably the last officers of Guard Regiment *Grossdeutschland* to experience the capitulation in the Reich capital. Shortly after midnight on 2 May, signals were sent by General Weidling, commandant of Berlin, from an LVII Panzer Army Corps radio unit near the command post: 'This is LVII German Panzer Corps. We request you cease fire. At 1230 Berlin time we will send negotiators to the Potsdamer Bridge. Recognition signal white flag ahead of red light. We request answer. We are waiting. This is LVII Panzer Corps . . .' The signal was repeated five times before the Soviets responded at 0530 and the capitulation followed on 2 May 1945.

---

* This was the colloquial German name for the feared Katyusha multiple rocket launcher. The weapon, which was mounted on the back of a truck, not only resembled a church organ but also made a fearsome groaning whine as it fired. Hence 'Stalin organ'.

At the Guard Regiment *Grossdeutschland* barracks in Berlin, Captain Hoss gathered the last of his men around himself and told them: 'The city of Berlin has surrendered!' In silence, buckles were released, weapons and ammunition cast aside. Some of the spirit left the men. The battle was over.*

After Weidling surrendered the Berlin garrison, Stalin issued the following order of the day:

The troops of the 1st Byelorussian Front commanded by Marshall Zhukov, in cooperation with the 1st Ukrainian Front commanded by Marshall Ivan Koniev, completed the destruction of the German Army Group in Berlin after bitter street fighting, and today, 2 May 1945, Berlin, capital of Germany, the centre of German imperialism and the home of German aggression, has been fully occupied. At 1500 hrs Moscow time the head of defence for Berlin, General der Artillerie Weidling, and his staff leaders abandoned resistance and ordered the garrison defending the city to lay down their weapons and give themselves as captives. At 2100 hrs more than 70,000 German officers and men had been taken prisoner by our troops. To mark the victory, those units that distinguished themselves especially in the battle to conquer Berlin will bear the name Berlin in future and receive decorations. Today, 2 May 1945, in the name of the Homeland, the capital of our Homeland Moscow honours the heroic troops of the 1st Byelorussian and the 1st Ukrainian Front by firing a 324-gun salute, twenty-four rounds each gun, to mark this historic event, the conquest of Berlin. For this outstanding operation, I express my thanks to the troops of the 1st Byelorussian and the 1st Ukrainian Front, which participated in the struggle to conquer Berlin. Eternal fame to the heroes who in the fight for freedom and independence fell for our Homeland!

* Helmuth Spaeter, *Die Geschichte der Panzerkorps Grossdeutschland*, Duisburg 1958, pp.748ff.

The price that the Red Army paid for Berlin was very high. From 16 April to 8 May, skirmishes continued to flare after the capitulation: the 1st and 2nd Byelorussian Fronts and the 1st Ukrainian Front lost 304,887 men dead, missing and wounded, 2,156 tanks and SP guns, 1,220 field guns and mortars were destroyed and 527 aircraft shot down.

The remnants of Major General Bärenfänger's group assembled in Humboldthain Park in broad daylight; they were fully armed and equipped. There was indecision. Bärenfänger convened a soldiers' council, at which it decided to abandon resistance. All weapons, including the panzers, were destroyed.

Meanwhile the Mohnke group had hidden in the ruins near Stettiner station. Towards 0700 on 2 May, they set off for Wedding, where the worried women of the town emerged to assist the SS men and shared the last of their food with them. From there the group moved on to the nearby Schultheiss–Patzenkofer Brewery, which was crowded with soldiers. The Russians had not yet been in this neighbourhood. Officers and men waited in inactivity. Finally Mohnke sent Colonel Clausen to reconnoitre; he returned with news of Weidling's surrender and the establishment of contact with the Russians. It was now evening. The conversation was limited to considerations of whether one should shoot oneself. Earlier, the women (except Hitler's dietician-cook Konstanze Manziarly who vanished mysteriously from the group) had got through to the west, led by an unknown sergeant.

In the brewery the discussion became ever more heated, especially when twenty-four-year old SS-Obersturmführer Stehr stated: 'Others may surrender, but Waffen-SS officers should not survive the death of the Führer.' At that moment a Soviet negotiator appeared. Dr Schenck described the dramatic minutes following:

> The negotiator was followed by a Russian officer and four men. As they came through the entrance there were two loud reports inside

the room. Hewel had put a pistol to his temple and squeezed the trigger as he bit on a cyanide capsule. I went to him immediately: he was dead. I could see it at a glance.

The thought struck me at once that this was how Hitler had died and Hewel had copied him, biting on a cyanide capsule and shooting himself at the same instant. I needed no second look. I went to the other man, Stehr. He was dead, his damaged head propped against the field bed.[*]

For the rest of them surrendering on 2 May, there now began long years of captivity.

After all groups had left the Führer-bunker, the dead waiting to be found and removed were: General Hans Krebs, General Wilhelm Burgdorf and SS-Obersturmbannführer Fritz Schädle (the seriously wounded leader of Hitler's personal bodyguard), all of whom had committed suicide, as well as the six Goebbels children. Two men had remained voluntarily: the telephone operator SS-Oberscharführer Rochus Misch and machinery plant supervisor Johannes Hentschel. Misch left the bunker around three in the morning once everything had been closed down, and was captured shortly afterwards by the Soviets. Hentschel stayed back. He was one of the Old Reich Chancellery staff kept on after 1933. Even though not a Party member, he enjoyed Hitler's confidence. In the final days of the Third Reich he had the vital task to perform – a duty he fulfilled faithfully – of keeping the diesel generator running. It supplied the Führer-bunker with electric current and amongst other things worked a water pump near the bunker dressing station. Here there were more than 300 wounded under the care of Dr Werner Haase, who was himself seriously ill and who struggled on alone after Dr Schenck left with a break-out group. Haase told Hentschel

---

[*] Ernst-Günther Schenck, *Ich Sah Berlin Sterben*, Herford 1970, p.159.

that if the light and water failed the wounded would die. Thus the non-Party man, the civilian Hentschel, remained at his post without a word of protest. Suppressing his fears, he worked on alone in the company of the dead, and held out in the most dangerous place in the collapsed German Reich.[*]

This fact is somewhat embarrassing for Soviet historians, for it exposes the Soviet version of what happened when they got to the Führer-bunker to derision. The official Communist Party *History of the Great Patriotic War* reported that Lieutenant Colonel Ivan Klimenko was the first Russian to enter the bunker. For this heroic deed he was proclaimed a 'Hero of the Soviet Union'. Commissar Klimenko was head of the 79th Rifle Corps SMERSH unit under Lieutenant General Pereviorkin. He came with a mission from the Soviet secret service.

Lev Bezymenski, the Soviet historian, recorded this statement by Klimenko:

As 79th Rifle Corps had captured the Reichstag, my unit was housed in the buildings of Plötzensee prison; all Wehrmacht members made prisoner from the Reichstag and Reich Chancellery sectors were brought here. Naturally we questioned them about the fate of the leaders of the Fascist Reich, principally Hitler and Goebbels. Some of them stated they had heard both committed suicide in the Reich Chancellery. On 2 May I went with four witnesses to the Reich Chancellery. It was after midday and raining. I got into the jeep, the witnesses and soldiers went in the truck. We parked outside the Reich Chancellery, went into the gardens and arrived at the emergency exit to the Führer-bunker. Just as we approached one of the Germans shouted: 'That is the body of Goebbels! That is the body of his wife!' I decided to take these bodies with us. As we had no stretchers, we put the bodies on a torn-off door, loaded

---

[*] Bahnsen & O'Donnell, *Die Katakombe*, pp.349ff.

them into the truck and returned to Plötzensee. Next day we found the bodies of the six Goebbels' children and General Krebs in the bunker. They were also taken to Plötzensee.

Later generals and officers from the staffs of the Third Assault Army and the 1st White Russian Front arrived, together with Soviet war correspondent Martyn Mershanov and Boris Gorbatov. Now began the identification procedure. It went ahead as follows: Goebbels's body was on the table in one room, the bodies of his wife and children, and that of General Krebs were laid on the floor. The witnesses were in the other room. The first to enter was Vice Admiral Voss, Dönitz's representative at FHQ: he had been captured by members of Third Assault Army signals service. Without hesitation, he identified Goebbels and his children. The other witnesses did the same.*

Soviet historians were therefore left in the dark by their 'brave' SMERSH colleagues, who had overlooked machinery operator Hentschel in the Führer-bunker working the diesel generator. At about 0900 hrs on 2 May, Hentschel heard Russians voices in his machinery room. Automatically he supplied light to the entire bunker. To his surprise he saw about a dozen Soviet female doctors in uniform carrying large sacks. They asked Hentschel about Hitler. After he told them that Hitler was dead, their interest turned to Hitler's wife. After Hentschel had told them that she too was dead, one of the female doctors who spoke good German got to the nitty-gritty: 'Where is her wardrobe?' Hentschel led the doctors to Eva Hitler's room, where they made short work of emptying the closets of the two deceased, Eva Hitler and Frau Goebbels.

When Hentschel returned to his machinery room at about ten, he was menaced by two Russian officers with drawn pistols: a major who spoke Hebrew and a captain. The captain put his pistol to

---

* Lev Bezymenski, *Der Tod des Adolf Hitler*, Hamburg 1968, pp.51f. Published in English as *The Death of Adolf Hitler*, London 1968.

Hentschel's head and cocked the hammer for fun, then with a smile drew a knife across Hentschel's throat but without drawing blood. They were both interested in Hitler, and Hentschel repeated what he had told the female doctors who, at that moment, were making their way in triumph down the corridor, sacks full of ladies' lingerie and dresses, and passed the two Russian officers. Finally the major ordered Hentschel to open the nearest door. This was the Goebbels' room in which the bodies of their small children lay. The Russians recoiled in horror and left the bunker pensively.*

The American historian Cornelius Ryan investigated this trail very closely, and while researching for his well-known book *The Last Battle* in the Soviet Union he came across Major Boris Polevoi, completely overlooked by Soviet official history. Polevoi, now a colonel, told Ryan that he had been in the Führer-bunker at 1030 on 2 May 1945. Ryan wrote:

> Although the Russians knew that the Führer-bunker was below the Reich Chancellery, it took them several hours to find it. The Red soldiers looking for it asked German passers-by on the street to take them there. Photographer Gerhard Menzel had never heard of the bunker, but accompanied a group of soldiers inside the ruined Reich Chancellery. Russian pioneers with mine-searching equipment went into the labyrinth of cellars and corridors first. Once a room had been swept, other soldiers collected up documents, files and letters. Suddenly the Russians gave Menzel a pair of binoculars and sent him on his way. They had reached the actual Führer-bunker.
>
> First of all they came across the bodies of Krebs and Burgdorf in a sitting position at a long table with many glasses and bottles. This was in the waiting area of the corridor. Both had shot themselves: they were identified by documents in their uniforms. Major Polevoi,

---

* Johannes Hentschel in Bahnsen & O'Donnell, *Die Katakombe*, pp.375ff.

attached to one of the first search teams, went quickly through the entire bunker.*

So why was Klimenko declared a 'Hero of the Soviet Union' for entering the Führer-bunker first when he was obviously at least the third to go in? There was a good reason. Stalin had long been aware that the victorious Red Army, or rather its popular generals, were in an excellent position to endanger his unlimited dictatorship. Before the anticipated end of the war he had decided to act by the maxim 'divide and rule' and had put rivals Zhukov and Koniev into competition with each other for the final battle for Berlin. Polevoi, attached to Koniev's army, had strayed across the demarcation line into Zhukov's sector, and took care to remove himself quietly. Thus Klimenko, attached to Zhukov's army, found an open road to rank and honours.

The precautions taken by SMERSH-Commissars in the Führer-bunker are understandable. Many German battle groups had not received notice of the break-out or of Weidling's capitulation, and were fighting on tenaciously. About eighty men of a Latvian group under SS-Sturmführer Neilands had been forgotten, together with the last French group of SS-Division *Charlemagne*. Wounded SS-Unterscharführer Scholl reported:

I have no idea for how long I was out, but I woke to the dreaded words: 'Move off!' There was utter confusion. Everybody moved off. There was actually no place to move off to, for behind us, in front of us, to the right and left of us and perhaps above us on the street too there were Russians. Nevertheless everybody was flooding out. Heading north.

I lay helpless on my stretcher, pleading and shouting for them to take me along. Two despatch riders from SS-Regiment

---

* Cornelius Ryan, *The Last Battle*, p.410.

Danmark came by. They promised not to leave me in the lurch, found two comrades and carried me. On the way they came across a small rail trolley on which they laid me and pushed it along the subway tracks. At Französische-Strasse station they worked it into a siding. Everything came to a stop again. My pain had gone and I fell asleep.

When I awoke it was the same picture, a great crowd of soldiers with no idea what to do next. It grew light above, 2 May dawned. Suddenly a loud voice made itself heard: 'Men! The Russians are in front of us, before, above and behind us. A Russian commissar is ordering us to surrender. Comrades, shall we give ourselves up?' Shouts of 'Yes!' and 'No!' Heated debates. Agreement. Dissent. An officer requested all officers present to come forward for talks with the commissar. Then came the decision. 'Comrades! Berlin is already behind enemy lines. The city commandant has signed the capitulation. Even the last outposts of resistance have given in. Russian tanks are in every street. Attempts to break through will fail. All soldiers of the Waffen-SS, Wehrmacht and Volkssturm are laying down their arms and being considered prisoners of war. Women, children and civilian males can go home. The wounded will be treated in a military hospital. Nobody should do anything stupid!' I accepted this order with nonchalant indifference.

Everybody headed slowly for a shaft up to Französische-Strasse. They pushed my trolley along. There was a seriously wounded man beside me. Some committed suicide: one pistol shot after another. The remainder climbed up, leaving the wounded behind. I saw some Russians approaching from some distance away, illuminating the tunnel with their flash lamps. A Russian pushed my trolley forwards, pausing to frisk the dead as we passed them. Slowly a mountain of pistols, watches, rings, anything valuable, built up on our trolley. The Russian was talkative. 'Germany finished. Hitler finished. You hospital and then home!' he said for the umpteenth time. Close to the ladder he stopped the trolley, took the booty and left us to our fate. Despite my leg wound, I got off the trolley, went forward on all fours to the ladder and dragged myself up in terrible pain.

Our men were heading northwards. Russians were milling around everywhere. I reached the surface a few metres from Unter den Linden station. It was cold and wet. I was freezing and sat on the remains of a wall in exhaustion. Friedrich-Strasse and Unter den Linden had lively traffic. No more sound of fighting was to be heard.*

Tragically, in isolated areas, the bitter fighting continued into 3 May. Soviet loudspeaker vans with German announcers raced through the streets of rubble, making known the capitulation and ceasefire. Hesitantly the last German fighting groups put aside their weapons. The battle was over.

In the Battle for Berlin about 150,000 civilians lost their lives, principally to Soviet bombing and shelling. Some 20,000 succumbed to illness and disease, mostly heart-attacks, while 6,000 Berliners committed suicide after the Russian victory and around 100,000 females from a tender age upwards were raped by Russian soldiers.

* Gosztony, *Der Kampf um Berlin 1945*, pp.384ff.

Appendix 3

Christa Schroeder's He Was My Chief

Publisher's Note

Readers of *I Was Hitler's Chauffeur: The Memoirs of Erich Kempka* may also enjoy Heinz Linge's *With Hitler to the End* (Frontline Books, 2009) and Christa Schroeder's *He Was My Chief* (Frontline Books, 2009). The following extracts are taken from Schroeder's memoir.

WHEN REPLYING TO A tiny job advertisement in the German newspaper, *Münchner Neuesten Nachrichten*, I had no premonition that it was to determine the future course of my life. It was 1930, and aged 22, I had just arrived in Munich from Bavaria, eager to explore a new part of Germany. The post was a secretarial one and I was invited by an unknown organisation, the 'Supreme SA leadership (OSAF)' to present myself in the Schellingstrasse. In this almost unpopulated street the Reich leadership of the NSDAP, the Nazi Party, was located at No. 50 on the fourth floor of a building at the rear.

That the post was awarded to me, someone who was neither a member of the NSDAP nor interested in politics nor aware of whom Adolf Hitler might be, must have resulted purely from my being a 22-year-old with proven shorthand/typing experience who could furnish good references.

Once Hitler had become Reich Chancellor, stenotypists were requested to volunteer for the NSDAP Liaison Staff in Berlin. In March 1933 I arrived in the capital.

*

After seizing power, Hitler had installed himself in Berlin's Radziwill Palace. His study, the library, his bedroom and later, alongside it, Eva Braun's apartment were all on the first floor.

Directly opposite the door to Hitler's study a couple of steps led to a long corridor, beyond which was the so-called adjutancy wing with the rooms for Hitler's aides. The first room was the Staircase Room (Treppenzimmer), where at least one of us would be permanently on standby, should Hitler need to give a dictation. Then came the rooms of Julius Schaub, Hitler's rather unprepossessing factotum, Dr Dietrich (Reich press officer), Sepp Dietrich (commander of *SS-Leibstandarte* Adolf Hitler, Hitler's personal bodyguard unit) and Hitler's chief adjutant, Wilhelm Brückner.

If one descended the staircase beyond these one came to the so-called ladies' saloon, actually the reception room, to the left of which wing doors, always pegged open, led into the film room. To the right was the Bismarck Room, also known as the smoking room. The dining hall was next to it and annexed to the Winter Garden, which ended in a fine semicircular path. Breakfast was taken in the Winter Garden and in the afternoon Hitler held most of his talks strolling its length.

One day Hitler happened to pass the Staircase Room at teatime, saw us sitting there and asked if he might join us. This hour of easy chatter was so much to his liking that he later came to tea almost daily. The Staircase Room was a place where he felt unburdened and I always had the impression that what he said there came from a secret memory box which at all other times he kept locked shut.

He would often recall pranks played in late childhood, for example, the time as a 12 year old when he wagered his classmates that he could make the girls laugh during a religious service. He won the bet by intently brushing his non-existent moustache.

He also spoke of his mother, to whom he was very attached, and of his father's violence: 'I never loved my father,' he used to say, 'but feared him. He was prone to rages and would resort to violence. My poor mother would then always be afraid for me. When I read Karl May once that it was a sign of bravery to hide one's pain, I decided that when he beat me the next time I would make no sound. When it happened – I knew my mother was standing anxiously at the door – I counted every stroke out loud. Mother thought I had gone mad when I reported to her with a beaming smile, "Thirty-two strokes father gave me!" From that day I never needed to repeat the experiment, for my father never beat me again.'

*

I found Hitler's eyes expressive. They could look friendly and warm-hearted, or express indignation, indifference and disgust. In the last months of the war they lost expressiveness and became a more watery, pale light blue, and rather bulging. One could always tell his mood from his voice. It could be unusually calm, clear and convincing, but also excited, increasing in volume and becoming overwhelmingly aggressive. Often it would be ice-cold. 'Ice-cold' or 'Now I am ice-cold' were much-used phrases of his. 'I am totally indifferent to what the future will think of the methods which I have to use,' I heard frequently. 'Ruthless' (rücksichtslos) was common in his vocabulary: 'Force it through ruthlessly, whatever the cost!'

Hitler's nose was very large and fairly pointed. I do not know whether his teeth were ever very attractive, but by 1945 they were yellow and he had bad breath. He should have grown a beard to hide his mouth. During the years of his friendship with Ada Klein, who worked on the Nazi party newspaper, *Völkischer Beobachter*, he told her: 'Many people say I should shave off the moustache, but that is impossible. Imagine my face without a moustache!' and at that held his hand below his nose like a plate. 'My nose is much too big. I need the moustache to relieve the effect!'

*

In 1978, Henriette Schirach [the wife of Baldur Benedikt von Schirach, head of the Hitler youth and Reich governor of Vienna during the Nazi occupation] reminded me of an encounter she had with Hitler on Good Friday, 1943. I remember that evening. While the other guests were talking, an argument developed between Henriette and Hitler, the subject of which was an occurrence in Amsterdam a few days previously. She had been awoken at night by an unusually loud disturbance and had watched from a hotel window as some weeping women were ordered forward across a bridge and disappeared into the night.

The next day she learned from her friends that this had been a deportation of Jewish women. She promised to bring the matter to the attention of Hitler, which she was now doing. Hitler answered her in a very brusque manner: 'Be silent, Frau von Schirach, you understand nothing about it. You are sentimental. What does it matter to you what happens to female Jews? Every day tens of thousands of my most valuable men fall while the inferior survive. In that way the balance in Europe is being undermined,' and here he moved his cupped hands up and down like a pair of scales.

'And what will become of Europe in one hundred, in one thousand years?' In a tone which made it evident that he considered the matter closed, he declared: 'I am committed by duty to my people alone, to nobody else!'

Index

Other books on the Second World War published by
Frontline include:

AT ROMMEL'S SIDE
The Lost Letters of Hans-Joachim Schraepler
Edited by Hans-Albrecht Schraepler
Introduction by Dennis Showalter
ISBN 978-1-84832-538-8

CHURCHILL'S UNDERGROUND ARMY
A History of the Auxiliary Units in World War II
John Warwicker
Foreword by Lord Ironside
ISBN 978-1-84832-515-9

COUNTDOWN TO VALKYRIE
The July Plot to Assassinate Hitler
Nigel Jones
Afterword with Count Berthold Schenk von Stauffenberg
ISBN 978-1-84832-508-1

THE DEVIL'S WORKSHOP
A Memoir of the Nazi Counterfeiting Operation
Adolf Burger
ISBN 978-1-84832-523-4

ESCAPE FROM THE THIRD REICH
Folke Bernadotte and the White Buses
Sune Persson
Preface by Brian Urquhart
ISBN 978-1-84832-556-2

THE GESTAPO
A History of Horror
Jacques Delarue
ISBN 978-1-84832-502-9

HE WAS MY CHIEF
The Memoirs of Adolf Hitler's Secretary
Christa Schroeder
Introduction by Roger Moorhouse
ISBN 978-1-84832-536-4

HITLER'S ROCKETS
The Story of the V-2s
Norman Longmate
ISBN 978-1-84832-546-3

LAST DAYS OF THE LUFTWAFFE
German Luftwaffe Combat Units 1944-1945
Manfred Griehl
ISBN 978-1-84832-511-1

LAST DAYS OF THE REICH
The Diary of Count Folke Bernadotte, October 1944–May 1945
Count Folke Bernadotte
Introduction by Sune Persson
ISBN 978-1-84832-522-7

THE MEN WHO TRIED TO KILL HITLER
The Attempt on Hitler's Life in July 1944
Heinrich Fraenkel and Roger Manvell
Foreword by Roger Moorhouse
ISBN 978-1-84832-509-8

NO CLOAK, NO DAGGER
Allied Spycraft in Occupied France
Benjamin Cowburn
Introduction by M. R. D. Foot
Foreword by Sebastian Faulks
ISBN 978-1-84832-543-2

NOTES OF A RUSSIAN SNIPER
Vassili Zaitsev and the Battle of Stalingrad
Vassili Zaitsev
Foreword by Max Hardberger
ISBN 978-1-84832-565-4

REPORT ON EXPERIENCE
A Memoir of the Allies' War
John Mulgan
Introduction by M. R. D. Foot
Foreword by Richard Mulgan
ISBN 978-1-84832-554-8
Publication April 2010

SNIPER ACE
From the Eastern Front to Siberia
Bruno Sutkus
Introduction by David L Robbins
ISBN 978-1-84832-548-7

TAPPING HITLER'S GENERALS
Transcripts of Secret Conversations, 1942–1945
Sönke Neitzel
Foreword by Ian Kershaw
ISBN 978-1-84415-705-1

THE VENLO INCIDENT
How the Nazis Fooled Britain
Captain Sigismund Payne Best
Introduction by Nigel Jones
ISBN 978-1-84832-558-6

WITH HITLER TO THE END
The Memoirs of Adolf Hitler's Valet
Heinz Linge
Introduction by Roger Moorhouse
ISBN 978-1-84832-544-9